A

A&E departments and self-harm **199**.13-14
A-levels (Advanced Level) **139**.4
  'dumbing down' claims **139**.19-20
  and gender **139**.10; **154**.22-3, 26
  results **139**.18
  science **139**.21
abortion **171**.1-39
  access to abortion services **171**.33
    at GP surgeries **171**.25-6
    online advice **171**.36
  after-effects **171**.3, 4-5
  arguments against (pro-life) **171**.21-3, 31
  arguments for (pro-choice) **171**.32-3
  attitudes to **171**.8
  definition **152**.2
  early medical abortion **171**.26
  failure **171**.2-3, 4
  home abortions **171**.35-6
  and humanism **171**.19-21
  and the law **171**.1, 5-7
    and doctors' objections to abortions **171**.27-8
    Northern Ireland **171**.15-16
    and religion **171**.18
    worldwide **171**.11-12
  methods
    medical abortion ('the abortion pill') **171**.2, 35, 36
    surgical abortion (vacuum aspiration) **171**.2
    unsafe methods **171**.12
  reasons for abortions **171**.1
    disability **171**.22
    rape **171**.21-2
    to save mother's life **171**.23
  religious positions on **171**.17-19
  risks **171**.3, 4-5
  safety, worldwide **171**.11-12
  statistics **171**.11-12; **173**.3, 9; **182**.2, 29
  success rate **171**.2-3
  and teenage pregnancies **173**.3, 9; **182**.2, 12-13, 29
    making the decision **182**.6, 9
  time limit
    public opinion **171**.30
    reasons to keep at 24 weeks **171**.32-4
    reasons to reduce **171**.31
    women's opinions **171**.29
Abortion Act **171**.5, 7
absenteeism
  from school, gender differences **154**.25
  sickness absence **183**.8, 9
  and work-life balance **183**.17
absolute human rights **167**.2, 4
abstinence education **173**.37
abuse
  effect on children **166**.35
  and young people **155**.19-26
abusers
  domestic, help for **155**.33-4
  see also paedophiles
abusive videos (happy slapping) **165**.31
academic achievement *see* educational achievement
academies **139**.14-16
Acceptable Behaviour Contracts (ABCs) **177**.8
access rights, disabled people
  to goods and services **197**.21, 25
  public transport **197**.23
  to work **197**.21, 24
access to children *see* contact
access courses **139**.30
accident warning devices, cars **119**.19
accidents
  alcohol-related **176**.15
  child labour and work-related **99**.1
  falls, older people **159**.4, 6
  road accidents, children **119**.5, 28, 30-31
  young people **176**.4
achievement *see* educational achievement
acidification of oceans **193**.30
acne **176**.20
action plan orders **177**.17
active euthanasia **152**.5
active traffic management **119**.37-8

Volume numbers appear first (in bold) followed by page numbers; a change in volume number is preceded by a semi-**colon.**

Vol. 88 Food and Nutrition
Vol. 97 Energy Matters
Vol. 99 Exploited Children
Vol. 100 Stress and Anxiety
Vol. 119 Transport Trends
Vol. 129 Gambling Trends
Vol. 134 Customers and Consumerism
Vol. 138 A Genetically Modified Future?
Vol. 139 The Education Problem
Vol. 140 Vegetarian and Vegan Diets
Vol. 141 Mental Health
Vol. 142 Media Issues
Vol. 144 The Cloning Debate
Vol. 146 Sustainability and Environment
Vol. 147 The Terrorism Problem
Vol. 148 Religious Beliefs
Vol. 149 A Classless Society?
Vol. 150 Migration and Population
Vol. 151 Climate Change
Vol. 152 Euthanasia and the Right to Die
Vol. 153 Sexual Orientation and Society
Vol. 154 The Gender Gap
Vol. 155 Domestic Abuse

Vol. 156 Travel and Tourism
Vol. 157 The Problem of Globalisation
Vol. 158 The Internet Revolution
Vol. 159 An Ageing Population
Vol. 160 Poverty and Exclusion
Vol. 161 Waste Issues
Vol. 162 Staying Fit
Vol. 163 Drugs in the UK
Vol. 164 The AIDS Crisis
Vol. 165 Bullying Issues
Vol. 166 Marriage and Cohabitation
Vol. 167 Our Human Rights
Vol. 168 Privacy and Surveillance
Vol. 169 The Animal Rights Debate
Vol. 170 Body Image and Self-Esteem
Vol. 171 Abortion – Rights and Ethics
Vol. 172 Racial and Ethnic Discrimination
Vol. 173 Sexual Health
Vol. 174 Selling Sex
Vol. 175 Citizenship and Participation
Vol. 176 Health Issues for Young People
Vol. 177 Crime in the UK
Vol. 178 Reproductive Ethics

Vol. 179 Tackling Child Abuse
Vol. 180 Money and Finances
Vol. 181 The Housing Issue
Vol. 182 Teenage Conceptions
Vol. 183 Work and Employment
Vol. 184 Understanding Eating Disorders
Vol. 185 Student Matters
Vol. 186 Cannabis Use
Vol. 187 Health and the State
Vol. 188 Tobacco and Health
Vol. 189 The Homeless Population
Vol. 190 Coping with Depression
Vol. 191 The Changing Family
Vol. 192 Bereavement and Grief
Vol. 193 Endangered Species
Vol. 194 Responsible Drinking
Vol. 195 Alternative Medicine
Vol. 196 Censorship Issues
Vol. 197 Living with Disability
Vol. 198 Sport and Society
Vol. 199 Self-Harming and Suicide

activists and the media **142**.10
activity, physical
Acts of Parliament **131**.24
adaptive dysfunction **197**.6
addictions **141**.9-10
    cannabis **186**.1, 10-11, 29
    gambling *see* compulsive gambling
    drugs **163**.2
    to the Internet **142**.37; **158**.38-9
    nicotine **188**.10, 16
        children **176**.13
    online gaming **158**.39
    shopping **134**.13-14
addictiveness of gambling **129**.30
ADD *see* attention deficit disorder
ADHD (attention deficit and hyperactivity disorder) **141**.19; **176**.30
adoption **178**.14-16; **182**.6, 8-9; **191**.18-25
    adoption leave **183**.18
    adoption process **191**.18-19
    same-sex couples **153**.31-2, 34; **178**.9-10; **191**.22-5
adult children
    living with parents **180**.23; **181**.4-5; **191**.26
    supported by parents **191**.27-8
adult literacy rates, and child labour **99**.11-12
adulterous consumption **161**.8-9
adultery **166**.13-14
advance directives (living wills) **152**.2, 35-6
    and the Mental Capacity Act **152**.37
advance fee scams **134**.26-7
Advanced Highers **139**.4
advertising **134**.7-1
    and age **196**.20
    airbrushing and unrealistic body images **184**.23
    alcohol **194**.39
    benefits of **134**.9
    and children **134**.10, 12; **165**.22
    junk food **88**.10, 11, 19, 20, 35, 37
    online **158**.5
    radio **158**.6
    regulation **134**.7,10
    television **158**.5

    tobacco **188**.23
    using disabled model **197**.10
adware **158**.34
aesthetic surgery *see* cosmetic surgery
affirmative action **154**.36
affluence *see* wealth
affluenza **134**.5
affordable housing **181**.36
    in rural areas **181**.3
    shortage of **181**.6, 29
Africa
    AIDS programmes **164**.7
    and genetically modified crops **138**.23
    HIV/AIDS infection rates **164**.4
    press freedom **196**.2
    slavery **167**.20
African-Caribbean people **115**.5
    pupils, exclusion **115**.19
African communities in UK
    HIV prevention campaigns **164**.24-5
    late HIV diagnosis **164**.17
age
    and advertising **196**.20
    and alcohol consumption **176**.3, 14; **194**.1-2, 30
    and alcohol-related deaths **194**.13
    and career fulfillment **183**.6
    and child labour **99**.2
    and child soldiers **99**.29-30
    of criminal responsibility **177**.19
    and depression **190**.5, 22-3
    at divorce **191**.8
    and drinking behaviour, young people **194**.2
    employment and gender **154**.29
    and employment, young people **180**.20
    and fertility **178**.4
    of first drink **194**.3
    of first sexual intercourse **182**.1
    of foetal viability **171**.23-4, 29
    of immigrants **150**.8
    and IVF **178**.1, 19-20
    at marriage **166**.4, 6; **191**.1
    and risk of divorce **166**.28

Volume numbers appear first (in bold) followed by page numbers; a change in volume number is preceded by a semi-**colon.**

Vol. 88 Food and Nutrition
Vol. 97 Energy Matters
Vol. 99 Exploited Children
Vol. 100 Stress and Anxiety
Vol. 119 Transport Trends
Vol. 129 Gambling Trends
Vol. 134 Customers and Consumerism
Vol. 138 A Genetically Modified Future?
Vol. 139 The Education Problem
Vol. 140 Vegetarian and Vegan Diets
Vol. 141 Mental Health
Vol. 142 Media Issues
Vol. 144 The Cloning Debate
Vol. 146 Sustainability and Environment
Vol. 147 The Terrorism Problem
Vol. 148 Religious Beliefs
Vol. 149 A Classless Society?
Vol. 150 Migration and Population
Vol. 151 Climate Change
Vol. 152 Euthanasia and the Right to Die
Vol. 153 Sexual Orientation and Society
Vol. 154 The Gender Gap
Vol. 155 Domestic Abuse

Vol. 156 Travel and Tourism
Vol. 157 The Problem of Globalisation
Vol. 158 The Internet Revolution
Vol. 159 An Ageing Population
Vol. 160 Poverty and Exclusion
Vol. 161 Waste Issues
Vol. 162 Staying Fit
Vol. 163 Drugs in the UK
Vol. 164 The AIDS Crisis
Vol. 165 Bullying Issues
Vol. 166 Marriage and Cohabitation
Vol. 167 Our Human Rights
Vol. 168 Privacy and Surveillance
Vol. 169 The Animal Rights Debate
Vol. 170 Body Image and Self-Esteem
Vol. 171 Abortion – Rights and Ethics
Vol. 172 Racial and Ethnic Discrimination
Vol. 173 Sexual Health
Vol. 174 Selling Sex
Vol. 175 Citizenship and Participation
Vol. 176 Health Issues for Young People
Vol. 177 Crime in the UK
Vol. 178 Reproductive Ethics

Vol. 179 Tackling Child Abuse
Vol. 180 Money and Finances
Vol. 181 The Housing Issue
Vol. 182 Teenage Conceptions
Vol. 183 Work and Employment
Vol. 184 Understanding Eating Disorders
Vol. 185 Student Matters
Vol. 186 Cannabis Use
Vol. 187 Health and the State
Vol. 188 Tobacco and Health
Vol. 189 The Homeless Population
Vol. 190 Coping with Depression
Vol. 191 The Changing Family
Vol. 192 Bereavement and Grief
Vol. 193 Endangered Species
Vol. 194 Responsible Drinking
Vol. 195 Alternative Medicine
Vol. 196 Censorship Issues
Vol. 197 Living with Disability
Vol. 198 Sport and Society
Vol. 199 Self-Harming and Suicide

Issues

Annual Index
2010

Your one-stop reference guide to the ever-popular Issues series!

Complete A-Z index listings for all 67 Issues titles currently in print

A fully comprehensive research tool for your students

First published by Independence
The Studio, High Green, Great Shelford
Cambridge CB22 5EG

© Independence, 2010

ISBN 978 1 86168 571 1

Compiled by
Ann Shooter

Edited by
Lisa Firth

Typeset by
Andrew Young

Printed in Great Britain
MWL Print Group Ltd

Cover
All photos © Independence.

retirement age **183**.14-15
    and self-esteem **170**.16
    of smokers **188**.1
        age started smoking **188**.3
    and social identity, by neighbourhood **149**.23
    and stress levels **100**.13
    and voter turnout **131**.19
    voting age lowering **131**.28, 29, 30
age of consent **99**.25-6; **173**.1, 8, 11; **176**.21-2
age discrimination **159**.4, 8-13
    young people **159**.12
age ratings, video games **196**.17
age-related macular degeneration **144**.22
ageing
    ageing process **159**.1-2, 31-2
    attitude to **159**.14-15
    benefits of exercise **159**.33; **162**.12
    and health **159**.31-9
    effect of lifestyle **159**.33, 34
ageing population
    global **150**.33, 35; **159**.5, 6
    UK **150**.28, 29, 39; **159**.3
ageism *see* age discrimination
ageist bullying **165**.9
agriculture
    and animal welfare **169**.11-13
    and bioenergy **97**.18
    and child labour **99**.1, 2, 4; **167**.32
    coffee growers **157**.32, 33
    cotton farming **157**.34
    egg production **140**.38-9
    exotic animals **140**.30
    fairtrade *see* fair trade
    and food nutrition **88**.31-4
    and forests **146**.30
    free trade in agriculture **88**.33
    greenhouse gas production **151**.7
    land use **146**.25
    and migrant workers **150**.11
    organic **146**.25
    sustainable **146**.27
see also animal welfare; food production; genetically
    modified (GM) crops; organic farming
agri-environment schemes **146**.25
agro-chemicals **138**.4
aid **160**.34-9
    aid tying **157**.10
    attitudes to **160**.35-6, 37
    negative effects **160**.38-9
    UK spending on aid **157**.9-10
AIDS (Acquired Immune Deficiency Syndrome) **96**.7,
    17-22, 36-9; **164**.1, 2
    AIDS-related illnesses **164**.2
    anti-AIDS campaigns **164**.23-5
    and assisted suicide **152**.31
    and child labour **99**.3
    and child soldiers **99**.31
    'cures' **164**.37-8
    deaths from **96**.36
    and dementia **141**.7
    and drug abuse **163**.11

education programmes **96**.32
global funding **96**.39
global statistics **96**.17-18, 24, 30, 36, 38
older people as carers **159**.5
orphans **96**.39; **164**.6, 7
pandemic **96**.31
and parents of lesbians and gay people **153**.9
and the sexual exploitation of children **99**.24
tackling stigma and discrimination **96**.19, 39
treatments **96**.18, 20
    antiretroviral therapy (ART) **96**.36, 37, 38, 39;
        164.2-3, 8-9, 29, 30-32
    fixed dose combinations (FDCs) **96**.37
    vaccines **96**.33-4; 34-5, 36
UK statistics **96**.20-2
and young people **96**.24-6, 29
see also HIV (Human Immunodeficiency Virus)
air pollution **146**.35-6
    monitoring **146**.37
    and transport **119**.1, 15, 16, 31
air travel
    airport security and congestion **156**.1
    carbon dioxide emissions from **97**.25
    and carbon offsetting **151**.22, 33, 39
    disabled people **197**.12
    effects of **156**.21
    environmental impact **156**.21, 26
    and pollution **119**.16
    security **147**.32
    and UK travel trends **156**.3; **161**.32
al-Qaida **147**.7
alcohol **88**.7, 24
    and accidents **176**.15
    advertising **194**.39
    binge drinking *see* binge drinking
    consumption
        children **194**.25-6
        myths **194**.16
        reducing **194**.5, 16, 23
        social drinkers **194**.17
        women **194**.7
        young people **194**.1-2
    and crime **194**.19-20, 21, 29
    deaths related to **163**.11; **194**.13
    and domestic violence **155**.4
    drink spiking **194**.8-10
    drinking behaviour
        binge drinking **194**.22-3
        children **194**.25-6
        and knowledge of safe drinking guidelines **194**.34
        social drinking **194**.17
        young people **194**.2-3, 24
    and eating disorders **184**.16
    effects of **176**.4, 5, 15; **194**.6-7, 9, 22-3
        on appearance **194**.6
        on behaviour **194**.19-20
        effects on others **194**.15, 27-8
    health benefits of **194**.18
    health risks of **194**.6, 7, 15, 17, 18
        binge drinking **194**.22-3
        mental health effects **194**.6

social drinking **194**.17

    young people **194**.19

and the law

    24-hour drinking **194**.20

    see also drink-driving

and mental health **141**.34

and pregnancy **194**.14

and sex **173**.15

and smoking **188**.10

and stress **100**.27, 31, 37, 39

and students **185**.9, 10

underage drinking **176**.17-18; **194**.1-3, 25

    see also young people and alcohol

units of **176**.15; **194**.4-5, 14

    recommended limits **194**.8, 14, 18

alcohol abuse **194**.22-39

    and crime **194**.21, 29

    effects on family **194**.27-8

    help **194**.23

    and homeless people **189**.10-11, 13

    risks **194**.22-3, 27-8

    signs of **194**.30

    statistics **194**.30

alcolocks **119**.8-9

algae biofuels **151**.24-5

alien invasive species **193**.12

    UK **193**.38-9

alternative medicine

    definition **195**.1

    see also complementary and alternative medicine

alternative tourism **156**.24

aluminium recycling **161**.22, 27

Alzheimer's disease **141**.6; **159**.4, 36-9

    and animal experimentation **144**.34

    diagnosis using eye test **141**.19

Amazon forest destruction and cattle ranching **193**.14

ambulance trusts **187**.5-6

amino acids **140**.7, 23

amnesia **141**.11

amphetamines **163**.4-5, 25

amyloid beta alcohol dehydrogenase (ABAD) **159**.37

anabolic steroids **198**.29-30

anaesthesia, and animal experiments **169**.17

anal sex and conception **182**.4

analgesics **198**.28-9

anger

    anger management **199**.6

    and domestic violence **155**.4, 34

anger management and domestic abuse **155**.34

Anglicanism *see* Church of England

animal cloning **144**.30-39

    Dolly the sheep **144**.1, 15, 30-31, 32, 34, 39

    and factory farming **144**.35

    and food production **144**.36-9

    and milk production **144**.36-8, 39

    risks **144**.39

animal experiments **169**.14-26

    alternatives to **169**.19, 21, 23

    arguments against **169**.15-16, 19; **144**.34

    arguments for **169**.14-15, 18, 19, 22

    and genetically modified animals **144**.34; **169**.16, 17

    and humanism **140**.32-3

    and non-toxological procedures **169**.17

    public attitudes to **147**.20

    regulation of **169**.14, 20, 22

    statistics **169**.17

    and toxicological procedures **169**.17

    types of animals used **169**.14, 17

animal fat as food ingredient **140**.18

animal feed **88**.35-6

    GM content **138**.25, 26

animal-human embryos **144**.9, 11, 13, 14, 20

animal husbandry principles **169**.12

animal rights **169**.1-3

animal rights activists

    and animal experiments **169**.20

    terrorism **147**.20-25

animal sentience **140**.27-8; **169**.2-3

animal suffering **140**.32

    and animal experiments **169**.14-15, 16, 25

    emotional suffering **169**.2

    fur farming **169**.5

    intensively farmed chickens **169**.13

    and live transport **169**.10

Volume numbers appear first (in bold) followed by page numbers; a change in volume number is preceded by a semi-**colon**.

Vol. 88 Food and Nutrition

Vol. 97 Energy Matters

Vol. 99 Exploited Children

Vol. 100 Stress and Anxiety

Vol. 119 Transport Trends

Vol. 129 Gambling Trends

Vol. 134 Customers and Consumerism

Vol. 138 A Genetically Modified Future?

Vol. 139 The Education Problem

Vol. 140 Vegetarian and Vegan Diets

Vol. 141 Mental Health

Vol. 142 Media Issues

Vol. 144 The Cloning Debate

Vol. 146 Sustainability and Environment

Vol. 147 The Terrorism Problem

Vol. 148 Religious Beliefs

Vol. 149 A Classless Society?

Vol. 150 Migration and Population

Vol. 151 Climate Change

Vol. 152 Euthanasia and the Right to Die

Vol. 153 Sexual Orientation and Society

Vol. 154 The Gender Gap

Vol. 155 Domestic Abuse

Vol. 156 Travel and Tourism

Vol. 157 The Problem of Globalisation

Vol. 158 The Internet Revolution

Vol. 159 An Ageing Population

Vol. 160 Poverty and Exclusion

Vol. 161 Waste Issues

Vol. 162 Staying Fit

Vol. 163 Drugs in the UK

Vol. 164 The AIDS Crisis

Vol. 165 Bullying Issues

Vol. 166 Marriage and Cohabitation

Vol. 167 Our Human Rights

Vol. 168 Privacy and Surveillance

Vol. 169 The Animal Rights Debate

Vol. 170 Body Image and Self-Esteem

Vol. 171 Abortion – Rights and Ethics

Vol. 172 Racial and Ethnic Discrimination

Vol. 173 Sexual Health

Vol. 174 Selling Sex

Vol. 175 Citizenship and Participation

Vol. 176 Health Issues for Young People

Vol. 177 Crime in the UK

Vol. 178 Reproductive Ethics

Vol. 179 Tackling Child Abuse

Vol. 180 Money and Finances

Vol. 181 The Housing Issue

Vol. 182 Teenage Conceptions

Vol. 183 Work and Employment

Vol. 184 Understanding Eating Disorders

Vol. 185 Student Matters

Vol. 186 Cannabis Use

Vol. 187 Health and the State

Vol. 188 Tobacco and Health

Vol. 189 The Homeless Population

Vol. 190 Coping with Depression

Vol. 191 The Changing Family

Vol. 192 Bereavement and Grief

Vol. 193 Endangered Species

Vol. 194 Responsible Drinking

Vol. 195 Alternative Medicine

Vol. 196 Censorship Issues

Vol. 197 Living with Disability

Vol. 198 Sport and Society

Vol. 199 Self-Harming and Suicide

animal welfare **88**.32-3, 35-6; **140**.27-39; **169**.1-13
   and animal experiments **169**.20, 21, 25
   areas of concern **169**.4
   consumer attitudes **140**.14, 31, 33
   egg production **140**.38-9
   and films **196**.14
   the Five Freedoms **169**.12
   Freedom Food mark **140**.34
   and fur trade **169**.6
   and humanism **140**.31-3
   measuring **169**.4
   meat production **140**.13; **169**.10, 13
   organic farms **140**.35-6
   UK legislation on **169**.3, 4
Animal Welfare Act **169**.3, 4
   and films **196**.14
anniversaries and grief **192**.5, 10, 20
annual percentage rate (APR) **180**.26
anorexia nervosa **184**.1, 3-4, 38-9
   link with brain development **184**.28
anthropomorphism **169**.3
anti-bullying strategies
   cyberbullying **165**.25-6
   peer mentoring **165**.18
   schools **165**.1, 8, 25
   workplaces **165**.36, 38
anti-consumerism **146**.39
anti-depressant drugs **190**.10-11, 32-3
   and bipolar disorder **190**.10-11
   having little effect on mild depression **190**.36
   and seasonal affective disorder **190**.7
   and suicide **190**.24
   see also drug treatments for depression
anti-discrimination legislation **183**.13
anti-gay abuse, football **198**.26
anti-obesity campaigns, potential harm **184**.33
anti-psychotic drugs **190**.10
anti-racism laws *see* legislation and racism
anti-retroviral therapy (ART) **96**.36, 37, 38, 39; **164**.2-3,
    8-9, 29, 30-32
   during pregnancy **164**.29-30, 31
   worldwide access to **164**.39
anti-social behaviour **177**.8
   and alcohol **194**.19-20
Anti-Social Behaviour Orders (ASBOs) **177**.8, 18, 25, 36-7
anti-social driving habits **119**.9
anti-terrorism measures
   legislation **147**.2, 3, 27, 35-6
   Muslims' views on **115**.34
   public attitudes to **167**.24
antibiotics **88**.14
   and organic farming **140**.35
   resistance to **138**.4
    and genetically modified organisms **138**.13
antiretroviral therapy (ART) **96**.36, 37, 38, 39
anxiety
   dangers of severe **100**.21
   defining **100**.21
   and depression **100**.24
   and mortality **190**.20
   and stress **100**.2, 21

   symptoms of **100**.21
appearance
   effects of alcohol **194**.6
   young smokers' concerns **188**.14
Applied AS awards **139**.18
apprenticeships **183**.29, 38
aquaculture (fish farming) **146**.29
armed conflict
   and the sexual exploitation of children **99**.20-1
   war-affected children **99**.32-3
   see also child soldiers
armed forces
   homelessness of ex-service personnel **189**.6
aromatherapy and stress relief **100**.37
arranged marriages **166**.16
arrests
   at football matches **198**.13
   your rights **177**.35-6
arthritis, young people **197**.16–17
artificial wombs **178**.1-2
arts-in-health movement **141**.38
arts therapies **141**.38
AS-levels (Advanced Supplementary levels) **139**.4, 18
asbestos disposal **161**.23
ASBOs (Anti-Social Behaviour Orders) **177**.8, 18, 25, 36-7
Asian people
   British identity **115**.37
   in football **198**.24
assault, equal protection for children **167**.36-9; **179**.31-2
assertiveness **170**.10
assertiveness training and stress **100**.32
Assisted Dying bill **152**.16, 17, 33
assisted reproductive technologies (ART) **178**.11-12
   ethical concerns **178**.11-12
   health problems for twins **178**.21-2
   see also in vitro fertilisation
assisted suicide **152**.1, 3, 5, 8-9
   arguments against **152**.20-21
   arguments for **152**.20
   and disabled people **152**.20-21; **199**.39
   legal guideline **199**.37-8
   and palliative care **152**.22
   physician-assisted suicide **152**.5, 7-8, 29-30, 31
asthma
   and exercise **198**.23
   increasing **119**.13, 26, 31
asylum seekers **150**.23
   asylum claims **150**.4, 23
   dawn raids **167**.27
   destitution **189**.14-15
   and HIV **96**.39
atheist protest against religious faith **196**.11-12
athletes
   drinking behaviour of stars, effect on young people **198**.14
   and drugs *see* drugs in sport
   punishment for missing drugs tests **198**.39
   talent identification **198**.8-10, 22
attempted suicide
   and stress in young people **100**.4
Attendance Allowance **197**.32-4
attendance centre orders **177**.17, 26

attention deficit and hyperactivity disorder (ADHD) **141**.19; **176**.30
auctions and consumer rights **134**.20
Australia, Internet censorship **196**.20
Australian Privacy Charter **168**.1-2
Autoclave waste sorting system **161**.25
autonomy **152**.6
 effect of legalising euthanasia **152**.6
 loss of, disabled people **152**.20
 and right to die **152**.3
aviation security **147**.32

B

babies
 and euthanasia debate **152**.4, 32, 33, 34
 and HIV **96**.31, 39
Bacillus cereus **88**.29
Bacillus thuringiensis (Bt) cotton **138**.35
backstreet abortions **171**.6, 22-3
bacteria **88**.27, 28-9
 transgenic **144**.11
bacterial vaginosis (BV) **173**.17
baculoviruses **138**.13-14
bail **177**.37
balance of excellence, sport **198**.37
balanced diet *see* healthy eating
banks **180**.25-7
 banking crisis **180**.4
 borrowing from **180**.26-7
 informing of a death **192**.32
 opening an account **180**.25
 and personal information **168**.8
 student accounts **185**.2-3
baptisms **148**.22
bariatric (weight loss) surgery **162**.3, 20
BASF GM potato trials **138**.27-8
batteries, recycling **161**.23, 28
battery eggs
 supermarket bans **140**.38
 see also free range eggs

Bayer CropScience, GM rice **138**.20, 31-4
BBC
 funding **142**.6
 Ofcom regulation **196**.20
 and portrayal of homosexuality **153**.24
bed and breakfast hotels, homeless families **189**.8
bees, declining numbers **193**.27-8
begging **189**.18-20
 children as beggars **99**.3, 4
 giving to beggars **189**.35-6
behaviour
 children, effect of poverty **160**.13
 effects of alcohol **194**.19-20, 23
 gender differences **154**.1, 9
 and poor body image **170**.19
 stress and behavioural changes **100**.33
Belarus, human rights abuses **167**.12-13
benefits *see* state benefits
benzene emissions **119**.15; **146**.36
bereavement **192**.1-39
 children **192**.4, 5-6,9-19, 21
 complicated **192**.16-17
 feelings **192**.1-2, 3, 9-10, 11
 funerals **192**.30-31, 34-7
 memorial websites **192**.38-9
 parents **192**.20-23
 practical matters **192**.24-39
 and stress in young people **100**.2
 support **192**.2, 4, 5-6
  children **192**.4, 5, 10, 17
  young people **192**.10, 12, 17
 young people **192**.9-19
betting **129**.2
bias and the media **142**.10
Big Issue **189**.37-9
bill payments and budgeting **180**.30-31
Bills (parliamentary) **131**.24
binding over **177**.18
binge buying **134**.13, 14
binge drinking **194**.22-3
 effects **176**.15; **194**.22-3
 young people **176**.14-16

binge eating 184.6-7, 35
bingo 129.2
binoculars, recycling 161.23
bioaccumulative chemicals 193.16
biochemical causes of depression 190.2
biodegradability of litter 161.16
biodiesel vehicles 119.21
biodiversity 146.18-21, 33
   and climate change 151.9
   and global economy 193.10-12
   key scientific questions 193.7
   loss 193.13
     England 193.31-2
   and oil palm industry 193.8-9
   protecting 146.20-21
   Scotland 146.21
   threats to 146.19, 21
   UK biodiversity Action Plan 146.33
   value of 146.18-19; 193.6
bioenergy 97.18
   biofuels 97.9; 138.4; 146.39; 151.24-5
   biomass 97.5, 6, 9, 11, 18
biological effects of compulsive gambling 129.29
biological attacks, response to 147.31
biological parents and parental responsibility 153.33
biological resources 146.9
   see also biodiversity
biology
   and gender development 154.1
   and sexual orientation 153.6, 7
biometrics
   biometric fingerprinting in schools 168.30
   biometric travel documents 168.13
   problems with 168.18
biotechnology
   definition 138.4
   public attitudes to 138.15-16; 144.19
bipolar affective disorder (manic depression) 141.14-15;
    185.8; 190.2, 8-11, 22
   causes 190.9
   diagnosis 190.8
   experiences of sufferers 141.28-9
   genetic factors 190.11, 12-13
   prevalence 190.23
   symptoms 190.8-9
   treatments 190.10-11
   types 190.9-10
birth country, non-white ethnic groups 115.38
   UK as birth country 131.8
birth rates
   and marital status 191.1
   to foreign parents in UK 150.29, 30
bisexuality 153.10-12
   definition 153.1
   discrimination 153.2
black box for road charging 119.36
black people
   church membership 148.23
   educational performance of children 115.19-20
   pupils 115.18-21; 139.9
bladder repair, stem cell therapy 144.21

blindness, disability classification 197.1
blogs 142.37; 158.3, 8
blood, effects of smoking 188.7
blood donation and HIV 164.1
blood doping 198.29
blood pressure *see* high blood pressure (hypertension)
blood products and HIV 96.14; 164.1, 19-20, 25
blood sports 169.27-39
blood sugar levels 88.15
blood tests
   drug testing in sport 198.27
   for HIV diagnosis 164.2, 20-21
   for mental illness diagnosis 141.18
BNP, inclusion in political debates 196.7, 8
boardroom positions, women 154.34
bodily privacy 168.2
body dysmorphic disorder/dysmorphophobia 170.29-30;
   184.7
body image 170.17-39; 184.17-24
   and bullying 165.8-9
   children 170. 21-2, 24
   definition 170. 17
   and exercise 141.39; 176.7
   and fashion industry 184.24
   girls 184.17-18, 27
   and sport 170.39
   improving 170.17, 20, 37-8
   and the media 170.22, 23, 24, 28, 30-31, 38
   men 184.20
   negative 170.17, 19-20
   positive 170.17, 37
   public concerns over 184.19-20
   and self-esteem 170.19
   and video games 170.27
body mass index (BMI) 88.8; 162.1, 4, 23
   and children 162.1
   criticism of 162.5
body weight 88.1, 12, 18
   and body image 170.19, 38
   and fertility 178.5
bonded labour 167.20, 32
bone marrow stem cells
   and heart disease treatment 144.23
   and sperm cell creation 144.29
bone marrow transplants 144.24
   saviour siblings 178.28-9
bones, effect of cannabis use 186.6, 29
books
   children's books and gay issues 153.19-20
   self-help books, mental health 190.38
border controls 147.29
borrowing
   from banks 180.26-7
boys and young men
   attitudes to sex 173.12-13
   and child labour 99.2
   child soldiers 99.31, 36
   and education 154.22-6
     foundation stage 154.23
     raising educational achievement 154.25
     single-sex teaching 154.26

subject choices **154**.22, 26
   underachievement **154**.23
and mental health problems **141**.1
and parenthood **182**.17
sexual exploitation of **99**.16, 21
street children **99**.19

brain
   brain development and anorexia risk **184**.28
   effects of cannabis on **186**.28-9
   effect of diet **141**.30-31
   and placebo effects **195**.28-9
   research, use of primates **169**.24-6
   stem cell therapy for brain damage **144**.22

brand awareness, children **134**.11
brand image and advertising **134**.8-9
brand names
   and bullying **165**.22
   as children's names **134**.12

Brazil
   cattle ranching and deforestation **193**.14
   censorship of sexual content on the Internet **196**.37

breast cancer and abortions **171**.3
breast surgery, teenagers **170**.32-3
Bretton Woods **157**.5
British Airways, carbon offsetting **151**.33
British Board of Film Classification (BBFC) **196**.13-16
   and legislation **196**.14
British history, importance of teaching **131**.7
British identity **131**.1-14; **156**.11
   Asians **115**.37
   and non-white ethnic groups **115**.38
British Medical Association (BMA)
   against NHS funding homeopathy **195**.16
   views on euthanasia **152**.1
British mentality and class **149**.6
British National Party, inclusion in political debates **196**.7, 8
British population
   ethnic groups **115**.3
   mixed-race relationships **115**.24
British tourists
   behaviour **156**.31
   visits abroad **156**.4

British Youth Council **131**.33
   and lowering voting age **131**.28
Britishness **131**.1-14
   decline of **131**.9
   effect of devolution **131**.5, 6
   and Islamophobia **131**.11
   and multiculturalism **131**.10
broadband services **158**.5-6, 17
   for low-income families **158**.18
broadcasting
   and freedom of expression **196**.24
   illegal **142**.7
   mergers **142**.4
   Ofcom regulation **196**.18-20
broadsheet newspapers **142**.8
brownfield sites **181**.36
BSE (bovine spongiform encephalopathy)
   and freedom of information **88**.14
Bt cotton **138**.35
BTecs, impact of specialist diplomas **139**.23-4
Buckinghamshire County Council, workplace travel plan **119**.32
Buddhism **148**.2
   festivals **148**.2
   food rules **148**.11
   funerals **192**.36
   meditation as treatment for depression **190**.35-6
Budget, the **180**.24
budgeting **180**.30-31
   for home buying **181**.24
   students **185**.3, 11
building industry *see* construction industry
building societies **180**.25-7
building waste recycling **161**.23
building your own home **181**.30-31
bulimia nervosa **184**.1, 4-5
bullfighting **169**.37-9
bullies
   characteristics of **165**.20, 21
   consequences for **165**.19, 26
   risk of suicide **165**.21-2
bullying **165**.1-39

Volume numbers appear first (in bold) followed by page numbers; a change in volume number is preceded by a semi-**colon.**

Vol. 88 Food and Nutrition
Vol. 97 Energy Matters
Vol. 99 Exploited Children
Vol. 100 Stress and Anxiety
Vol. 119 Transport Trends
Vol. 129 Gambling Trends
Vol. 134 Customers and Consumerism
Vol. 138 A Genetically Modified Future?
Vol. 139 The Education Problem
Vol. 140 Vegetarian and Vegan Diets
Vol. 141 Mental Health
Vol. 142 Media Issues
Vol. 144 The Cloning Debate
Vol. 146 Sustainability and Environment
Vol. 147 The Terrorism Problem
Vol. 148 Religious Beliefs
Vol. 149 A Classless Society?
Vol. 150 Migration and Population
Vol. 151 Climate Change
Vol. 152 Euthanasia and the Right to Die
Vol. 153 Sexual Orientation and Society
Vol. 154 The Gender Gap
Vol. 155 Domestic Abuse

Vol. 156 Travel and Tourism
Vol. 157 The Problem of Globalisation
Vol. 158 The Internet Revolution
Vol. 159 An Ageing Population
Vol. 160 Poverty and Exclusion
Vol. 161 Waste Issues
Vol. 162 Staying Fit
Vol. 163 Drugs in the UK
Vol. 164 The AIDS Crisis
Vol. 165 Bullying Issues
Vol. 166 Marriage and Cohabitation
Vol. 167 Our Human Rights
Vol. 168 Privacy and Surveillance
Vol. 169 The Animal Rights Debate
Vol. 170 Body Image and Self-Esteem
Vol. 171 Abortion – Rights and Ethics
Vol. 172 Racial and Ethnic Discrimination
Vol. 173 Sexual Health
Vol. 174 Selling Sex
Vol. 175 Citizenship and Participation
Vol. 176 Health Issues for Young People
Vol. 177 Crime in the UK
Vol. 178 Reproductive Ethics

Vol. 179 Tackling Child Abuse
Vol. 180 Money and Finances
Vol. 181 The Housing Issue
Vol. 182 Teenage Conceptions
Vol. 183 Work and Employment
Vol. 184 Understanding Eating Disorders
Vol. 185 Student Matters
Vol. 186 Cannabis Use
Vol. 187 Health and the State
Vol. 188 Tobacco and Health
Vol. 189 The Homeless Population
Vol. 190 Coping with Depression
Vol. 191 The Changing Family
Vol. 192 Bereavement and Grief
Vol. 193 Endangered Species
Vol. 194 Responsible Drinking
Vol. 195 Alternative Medicine
Vol. 196 Censorship Issues
Vol. 197 Living with Disability
Vol. 198 Sport and Society
Vol. 199 Self-Harming and Suicide

causes **165**.5
cyber-bullying **165**.2, 9, 23-31, 37-9
definitions **165**.1, 3-5
and eating disorders **184**.8
effects **165**.1, 19
fears of gay parents **153**.22
forms of **165**.3-5, 6, 8-9, 19
gender differences **154**.25
homophobic **153**.14-18; **165**.2, 9, 12-14
how to help **165**.6
in the community **165**.7-8
prevalence of **165**. 1-2, 18
reasons for **165**.1, 5, 18
risk factors **165**.3
school anti-bullying policies **165**.1, 8, 25
statistics **165**.1-2
and stress in young people **100**.1, 2, 4
and suicide **165**.20, 21-2
at work *see* workplace bullying
and workplace stress **100**.14, 15
burial
abroad **192**.31
natural **134**.31
bursaries, students **185**.2
bus travel
and disabled people **197**.11-12
and pollution **119**.12
trends **119**.1
bushmeat trade **193**.23
business ownership aspirations **183**.7
businesses
anti-terrorism measures **147**.32
and biodiversity protection **146**.20
and environmentalism **146**.38-9
and higher education **185**.34-6
sustainable **146**.7
butadiene **146**.36
butterflies, declining numbers, Britain **193**.36
buying a home
costs **181**.24
disability rights **197**.21-2
young people **181**.26

C

C.difficile **187**.28, 29
Cabinet, The **131**.21
CAFCASS (Children and Family Court Advisory and Support Service) **166**.26, 36
caffeine and mental health **141**.35
calcium **88**.6
dietary sources **140**.4; **176**.8
teenagers' requirements **176**.8
and vegetarian diets **140**.3
call barring **134**.28
calorie intake **88**.1, 12; **162**.8
teenagers **176**.8
CAMbrella, research into complementary medicine **195**.16
campaigns and the media **142**.10

campylobacter **88**.28
cancer
and alcohol consumption **194**.6
and cannabis use **186**.16, 15
and complementary therapies **195**.6-7
as disability **197**.1
leukaemia, stem cell therapy **144**.21
and passive smoking **188**.10-11
prevention **88**.17, 30
skin **176**.10-11
and smoking **188**.8-11
stem cell therapy for blood cancers **144**.21
and vegetarian diets **140**.9, 11
cancer treatments
and genetically modified hens **138**.20-21
cannabinoids
THC **186**.7, 9, 13, 22
cannabis **163**.6; **186**.1-39
appearance **186**.2
cannabis oil **186**.2, 7, 22
cannabis resin (hashish) **186**.2, 7, 9
chemical content **186**.7, 9
classification **186**.4-5, 32
see also reclassification
compulsive use **186**.11
cost **186**.2
cultivation **163**.25
method, effect on potency **186**.22
effects of **163**.6, 35-6; **186**.1, 3, 37-8, 9-10, 28-9
on bones **186**.6, 29
on the brain **186**.28-9
cancer healing claims **186**.16
on education and learning **186**.9-10
on family life **186**.23-5
on lungs **186**.15, 28
medicinal **186**.16-17
skunk **186**.13
forms of **186**.2, 7, 9
giving up **186**.11
and hard drug use **186**.29
herbal cannabis (marijuana/grass) **186**.2, 9
history **186**.3-4, 7, 16-17, 25
and the law **186**.1-2, 5, 8, 9, 30-39
legalisation debate **186**.4, 38-9
medicinal use of **186**.16-17
and mental health **163**.35; **186**.10-13, 16, 28-9, 30, 31, 32
names for **186**.1
penalties
for possession **186**.1-2, 5, 9, 30
for supply **186**.2, 30
potency of **186**.2, 6, 21, 22
skunk **186**.13
production *see* cannabis cultivation
psychosis **186**.10, 12, 31, 32
purity **186**.2-3
reclassification **163**.32, 35-6; **186**.4-5, 32-3
public opinion **186**.31
THC (delta-9 tetrahydrocannabinol) **186**.7, 9, 13, 22
use
Britain **163**.7
Europe **163**.25

giving up **186**.11

worldwide **186**.18-19

canned hunting **193**.17

cans, recycling **161**.27

canvassers **131**.18

capital flight **157**.5

car batteries, recycling **161**.28

carbohydrates **88**.2, 5-6, 15

carbon

carbon credits **151**.36-7

low carbon technologies **97**.4

carbon dioxide

atmospheric concentration **151**.7

CO2 equivalent **151**.13

rising levels, effects on oceans **193**.30

sources of **151**.4

carbon dioxide emissions

agriculture **151**.7

and air transport **97**.25

and biomass **97**.18

from fossil fuel burning **97**.1, 4

from power stations **97**.3

and global warming **151**.3

public awareness of **97**.34

reducing **97**.2; **151**.2, 13

from tourism **156**.25

from transport **119**.14, 15, 16, 24, 30

in the UK **97**.5, 21

see also greenhouse gas

carbon monoxide **146**.36

in tobacco smoke **188**.4, 7

transport emissions **119**.15

carbon offsetting **151**.20-22, 33-5; **156**.1

carbon sequestration **151**.26

carbon sinks **151**.26

carbon trading **151**.36-7

cardboard recycling **161**.24, 26-7

cardiology, stem cell therapy **144**.22, 23, 28

cardiovascular disease *see* heart disease

care funding, personalisation **197**.13

care homes **159**.27-8; **179**.10-11

care leavers

and homelessness **189**.6

housing rights **189**.25

care services for older people **159**.4

concerns about **159**.28

funding **159**.29

rising costs **159**.26

care trusts **187**.6

career advice

failing young people **183**.39

gender bias **154**.28, 35

career breaks **183**.18, 20

career fulfillment age **183**.6

carers

experiencing grief **192**.6

older people as carers **159**.4, 5

statistics **154**.30

carotenes **88**.2, 5

carrier bags *see* plastic bags

cars

attitudes to car use **97**.35, 36

batteries, recycling **161**.28

car clubs **119**.33

cleaner fuels **119**.20-23

congestion *see* congestion, traffic

dependency on **119**.7

emissions reduction **151**.39

fuel efficient **119**.20-24

ownership **119**.7, 11, 29

recycling **161**.23

reducing use of **119**.39

sharing **119**.32-3

speeding **119**.3, 4, 8

and pedestrian injuries **119**.5, 30-31

and speed cameras **119**.4, 17, 18

speed limiters **119**.18

spending on **134**.4, 25

tax and fuel efficiency **119**.24

usage trends **119**.1, 7-9, 11, 13, 29; **161**.31

see also road accidents

cartilage repair using stem cells **144**.21

cartons, recycling **161**.23

cartoons of Muhammed **142**.34

Volume numbers appear first (in bold) followed by page numbers; a change in volume number is preceded by a semi-colon.

Vol. 88 Food and Nutrition
Vol. 97 Energy Matters
Vol. 99 Exploited Children
Vol. 100 Stress and Anxiety
Vol. 119 Transport Trends
Vol. 129 Gambling Trends
Vol. 134 Customers and Consumerism
Vol. 138 A Genetically Modified Future?
Vol. 139 The Education Problem
Vol. 140 Vegetarian and Vegan Diets
Vol. 141 Mental Health
Vol. 142 Media Issues
Vol. 144 The Cloning Debate
Vol. 146 Sustainability and Environment
Vol. 147 The Terrorism Problem
Vol. 148 Religious Beliefs
Vol. 149 A Classless Society?
Vol. 150 Migration and Population
Vol. 151 Climate Change
Vol. 152 Euthanasia and the Right to Die
Vol. 153 Sexual Orientation and Society
Vol. 154 The Gender Gap
Vol. 155 Domestic Abuse

Vol. 156 Travel and Tourism
Vol. 157 The Problem of Globalisation
Vol. 158 The Internet Revolution
Vol. 159 An Ageing Population
Vol. 160 Poverty and Exclusion
Vol. 161 Waste Issues
Vol. 162 Staying Fit
Vol. 163 Drugs in the UK
Vol. 164 The AIDS Crisis
Vol. 165 Bullying Issues
Vol. 166 Marriage and Cohabitation
Vol. 167 Our Human Rights
Vol. 168 Privacy and Surveillance
Vol. 169 The Animal Rights Debate
Vol. 170 Body Image and Self-Esteem
Vol. 171 Abortion – Rights and Ethics
Vol. 172 Racial and Ethnic Discrimination
Vol. 173 Sexual Health
Vol. 174 Selling Sex
Vol. 175 Citizenship and Participation
Vol. 176 Health Issues for Young People
Vol. 177 Crime in the UK
Vol. 178 Reproductive Ethics

Vol. 179 Tackling Child Abuse
Vol. 180 Money and Finances
Vol. 181 The Housing Issue
Vol. 182 Teenage Conceptions
Vol. 183 Work and Employment
Vol. 184 Understanding Eating Disorders
Vol. 185 Student Matters
Vol. 186 Cannabis Use
Vol. 187 Health and the State
Vol. 188 Tobacco and Health
Vol. 189 The Homeless Population
Vol. 190 Coping with Depression
Vol. 191 The Changing Family
Vol. 192 Bereavement and Grief
Vol. 193 Endangered Species
Vol. 194 Responsible Drinking
Vol. 195 Alternative Medicine
Vol. 196 Censorship Issues
Vol. 197 Living with Disability
Vol. 198 Sport and Society
Vol. 199 Self-Harming and Suicide

cash cards **180**.13, 25
cash machine withdrawals **180**.16, 17
cash payments **180**.13
    statistics **180**.16-17
cashless society **180**.15-16
casinos **129**.2
    new, UK **129**.15, 34
    supercasino **129**.14-16, 34
casual sex, international comparisons **173**.6
catalogues and credit payment **134**.22
cathartic role of football **141**.32
Catholic Church
    and abortion **171**.17, 18
    and embryo research **178**.35
    and euthanasia **152**.11, 29
    and faith schools **148**.35
    and IVF **178**.17
cattle
    cloning **144**.36-8
    and hybrid embryos **144**.11
    ranching and deforestation **193**.14
    see also livestock farming
cautions **177**.36
CCTV (Closed Circuit Television) **168**.6, 7, 8-9, 22-5
    and anti-social behaviour **177**.8
    and crime prevention **168**.23-4
    in schools **168**.25
    and sound recording **168**.24
    statistics **168**.22
CDs, recycling **161**.23
celebrity culture
    and body image **170**.22
    and cosmetic surgery **170**.33
cell ageing **159**.1
cell nuclear replacement **144**.15
censorship
    films **196**.13, 14
    Internet **158**.37; **196**.27-39
    sexual content on the Internet **196**.36-8
census **150**.36
    ethnic group questions **115**.3
    religious affiliation results **148**.6-7
cereals **88**.5-6, 15
cerebral palsy **197**.3-4
certificates of identity **168**.13
cervical cancer
    screening **173**.39
    vaccination **173**.38-9
challenging racism **115**.2
    at work **115**.12
Chance to Shine cricket scheme **198**.3-4
character capabilities of children, factors affecting **191**.6-7
chatrooms
    and bullying **165**.24
    and sexual offences **158**.35
'chavs'
    children's perceptions of **149**.10-11
    prejudice against **149**.8
cheating in sport, childrens views on **198**.38
Chechen conflict and child soldiers **99**.37
cheese and vegetarian diets **140**.6, 18, 22, 26

chelation therapy **195**.5
chemical/biological incidents, response to **147**.31
chemicals
    disposal **161**.23
    impact on wildlife **193**.16-17
    in tobacco smoke **188**.4, 9-10, 15
cheques **180**.13, 25
chewing tobacco **188**.11
chickens, intensively farmed **169**.13
child abuse **179**.1-12
    and dependency **141**.10
    and dissociative disorders **141**.12-13
    emotional **179**.1; 5
    getting help **179**.5-6, 7
    help for professionals **179**.11-12
    and mental health problems **141**.10, 12-13
    neglect **179**.3, 5
        reporting **179**.7
        taking children into care **179**.10-11
    online **179**.15-16, 17; **196**.39
    physical **179**.1-2, 5
        see also corporal punishment; smacking
    prevalence **179**.4, 8-9, 13, 15, 17
    signs and symptoms **179**.5-6
Child Exploitation and Online Protection (CEOP) Centre **179**.15-16
Child Internet Safety, UK Council for (UKCCIS) **165**.30-31
child labour **99**.1-15; **167**.30-31, 32
    and age of child **99**.2
    attitudes to **99**.1
    combating **99**.11-13
    defining **99**.2, 3
    demand for **99**.3
    domestic work **99**.1, 4, 7-10
    economic benefits of eliminating **99**.1, 6, 15
    economic truths of **99**.14-15
    and education **99**.3, 7, 10, 11-12, 15
    and human rights **99**.4, 6
    impact on a child **99**.2, 3
    legislation and laws
        enforcement of **99**.11
        improving **99**.11
    organisations to take action against **99**.4
    and poverty **99**.2, 3, 4, 11, 12, 14-15
    reasons for **99**.1, 2-3, 3-4
    statistics **99**.1, 2, 14
    suitability for certain types of work **99**.4
    tobacco pickers **188**.39
    types of **99**.1, 2, 3, 4
child mortality, Milliennium Goals **160**.31
child pornography **99**.1, 16, 17, 20, 24, 25
    online **179**.17
child poverty **160**.2, 3, 11, 19, 25, 29
    public attitudes to **160**.14
    and education **160**.16-22
    and family debt **160**.12
    and women's poverty **160**.15
child prostitution **99**.1, 16, 17, 25-6, 27-8; **167**.32
child psychiatrists **100**.2
child safety orders **177**.18
child sex tourism **156**.37-9

child slavery **167**.20, 32-3
child soldiers **99**.1, 4, 29-39; **167**.32, 33-4
   age of **99**.29-30
   benefits of ending child soldier use **99**.39
   defining **99**.29
   girls **99**.29, 31, 36
   harmful effects of being **99**.31, 36
   and human rights atrocities **99**.30
   and non-governmental armed groups **99**.30
   statistics **99**.29
child trafficking **167**.32, 34
childbirth
   deaths in **154**.12
   and exercise **162**.32
childcare
   and children's development **191**.16-17
   financial help for young parents **182**.6
   and grandparents **191**.15, 16-17
   statistics **154**.30
childhood obesity **88**.3, 11; **162**.6, 13-14, 25-9; **176**.2, 3
   effects of exercise **162**.28, 29
   as neglect **162**.27
childhood problems
   and dependency **141**.9-10
   and post traumatic stress disorder **141**.3
   and suicide risk **199**.34
ChildLine
   and domestic violence **155**.25
   number of calls **181**.13
   peer support project (CHIPS) **199**.33
   and racism **115**.1
   and sex worries **173**.7
   and sexual abuse **179**.13-15
   and suicide **176**.35, 36-7; **199**.22, 31, 32, 33
children
   abuse *see* child abuse
   and advertising **134**.10, 12
   alcohol consumption **176**.3, 14; **194**.1-3, 25-6
      influence of household drinking habits **194**.25
   of alcoholic parents **194**.27-8
   anti-extremism education **147**.34
   attitudes to parents drinking **194**.28

attitudes to poverty **160**.4
and the beauty industry **170**.25-6
bereavement **192**.4, 5-6, 13-19, 21
   facts and figures **192**.12
   support **192**.4, 5-6, 10, 17
body image concerns **170**.21-2, 24
books showing gay couples **153**.19-20
and bullying **165**.3-5
in care, educational disadvantages **160**.22
of cohabiting couples **166**.14-15
communication trends **158**.4
and consumerism **134**.11-12
contact with parents after divorce **166**.37-8; **191**.11
costs of raising **134**.25
cricket scheme, improving social well-being **198**.3-4
cycling **119**.28, 30
death, children's understanding of **192**.4, 13, 15, 19
development, effect of childcare **191**.16-17
development of character capabilities **191**.6-7
disabled *see* disabled children
discipline *see* discipline
and divorce **166**.4-5, 29-31, 34-8; **191**.1, 9
and domestic violence **155**.1, 4, 5, 19-25
drug awareness **163**.27
earning money **180**.20
ethnic minorities, and education **115**.18, 19-21
exercise, lack of **162**.13, 15, 25
and food advertising **88**.10, 11, 20, 35, 37
and gambling
   online gambling **129**.18
   Scotland **129**.32-3
of gay couples **153**.20-22
gender development **154**.1
and grief **192**.4, 5-6, 19
health **176**.2-3
government strategy **162**.17
   and transport **119**.13-14, 31
healthy weight **162**.25
and HIV/AIDS **96**.20, 39; **164**.6-8
   preventing HIV transmission from mother **164**.25, 27, 29-30, 31
and homelessness **189**.29-32

Volume numbers appear first (in bold) followed by page numbers; a change in volume number is preceded by a semi-**colon.**

Vol. 88 Food and Nutrition
Vol. 97 Energy Matters
Vol. 99 Exploited Children
Vol. 100 Stress and Anxiety
Vol. 119 Transport Trends
Vol. 129 Gambling Trends
Vol. 134 Customers and Consumerism
Vol. 138 A Genetically Modified Future?
Vol. 139 The Education Problem
Vol. 140 Vegetarian and Vegan Diets
Vol. 141 Mental Health
Vol. 142 Media Issues
Vol. 144 The Cloning Debate
Vol. 146 Sustainability and Environment
Vol. 147 The Terrorism Problem
Vol. 148 Religious Beliefs
Vol. 149 A Classless Society?
Vol. 150 Migration and Population
Vol. 151 Climate Change
Vol. 152 Euthanasia and the Right to Die
Vol. 153 Sexual Orientation and Society
Vol. 154 The Gender Gap
Vol. 155 Domestic Abuse

Vol. 156 Travel and Tourism
Vol. 157 The Problem of Globalisation
Vol. 158 The Internet Revolution
Vol. 159 An Ageing Population
Vol. 160 Poverty and Exclusion
Vol. 161 Waste Issues
Vol. 162 Staying Fit
Vol. 163 Drugs in the UK
Vol. 164 The AIDS Crisis
Vol. 165 Bullying Issues
Vol. 166 Marriage and Cohabitation
Vol. 167 Our Human Rights
Vol. 168 Privacy and Surveillance
Vol. 169 The Animal Rights Debate
Vol. 170 Body Image and Self-Esteem
Vol. 171 Abortion – Rights and Ethics
Vol. 172 Racial and Ethnic Discrimination
Vol. 173 Sexual Health
Vol. 174 Selling Sex
Vol. 175 Citizenship and Participation
Vol. 176 Health Issues for Young People
Vol. 177 Crime in the UK
Vol. 178 Reproductive Ethics

Vol. 179 Tackling Child Abuse
Vol. 180 Money and Finances
Vol. 181 The Housing Issue
Vol. 182 Teenage Conceptions
Vol. 183 Work and Employment
Vol. 184 Understanding Eating Disorders
Vol. 185 Student Matters
Vol. 186 Cannabis Use
Vol. 187 Health and the State
Vol. 188 Tobacco and Health
Vol. 189 The Homeless Population
Vol. 190 Coping with Depression
Vol. 191 The Changing Family
Vol. 192 Bereavement and Grief
Vol. 193 Endangered Species
Vol. 194 Responsible Drinking
Vol. 195 Alternative Medicine
Vol. 196 Censorship Issues
Vol. 197 Living with Disability
Vol. 198 Sport and Society
Vol. 199 Self-Harming and Suicide

housing problems **181**.13, 14
inequality **167**.35
and the Internet **158**.20-21, 27-30
   watching pornography **196**.38
life on the streets **189**.27-8
in lone parent families **191**.12
and the mediation process **166**.39
and mental health
   mental health problems **141**.1, 20-21
   mental health programmes **141**.37
   effect of parents' mental health problems **141**.24-5
naming after brands **134**.12
obesity *see* childhood obesity
online gaming addiction **158**.39
online safety **165**.26-7, 30-31
and passive smoking **188**.5, 11
and parental relationships **166**.32; **191**.1
and parental separation **166**.4-5, 29, 30, 31, 32; **191**.1,
   8, 9
and poverty *see* child poverty
and prison *see* youth custody
and racism **115**.1-2, 9
and road accidents **119**.5, 28, 30-31
and road safety **119**.5-6
and self-esteem **170**.9-10
and self-harm **199**.17
sex, worries about **173**.7
slavery **167**.20-32-3
and smoking **176**.3, 12-13
   health effects **176**.12-13
   and the law **176**.13
   passive smoking **188**.5, 11
social differences, perceptions of **149**.9-12
and social housing **181**.9-11
and suicide **176**.35, 36-7
and terrorism **147**.32
time spent with fathers **191**.32
tobacco pickers, health problems **188**.39
travel to school **119**.26, 29-30
and women's careers **183**.21
and women's earnings **154**.35-6
children's rights **167**.28-39
and corporal punishment **167**.36-8; **179**.30, 31-2
statistics **167**.30
UN Convention on the Rights of the Child **167**.28-9
chimeras (human-animal hybrids) **144**.10-12
for stem cell research **178**.35
China
human rights **167**.23-4
Internet censorship **158**.37; **196**.27, 28, 29, 30
patriotic hacking of Internet **196**.34-5
receiving waste from UK **161**.17
UK dependence on **146**.4-5
Chinese medicine, risks **195**.36
chlamydia **173**.17, 20; **176**.25, 26
online testing for **173**.28
chocolate **88**.18-19, 31
vegan **140**.22, 26
choice as consumer right **134**.1
CHP (Combined Heat and Power) plants **97**.2, 4
Christianity **148**.2

and the Census (2001) **148**.6, 7
and church attendance **148**.7, 18-19, 20-21, 23, 27
degree of commitment **148**.7
denominations **148**.6
discrimination against **148**.28
festivals **148**.2
and food culture **148**.10
funerals **192**.34
Christmas church attendance **148**.19, 27
church attendance **148**.7, 18-19, 20-21, 23, 27
Church of England
baptisms **148**.22
and euthanasia **152**.34
and faith schools **148**.35
as state religion (established church) **148**.21-2
Church of Scotland and ethics of human cloning **144**.5-6
cigar smoking **188**.3
cigarettes
chemicals in **188**.4, 9-10, 15
consumption statistics **188**.3
cost **188**.15, 22
health warnings on packs ineffective **188**.29
packaging giving misleading messages **188**.20
circles of support, for sex offenders **179**.22-3
circus animals **169**.9-10
CITES (Convention on International Trade in Endangered
   Species) **146**.34; **193**.2
cities *see* cars, congestion; urban areas; urban growth
citizen photojournalism **142**.23
citizenship
British identity **131**.1-14
European Union **131**.38
global **131**.37
government **131**.15-25
survey **131**.2-3
test **131**.12
young people **131**.26-39
Citizenship Education in schools **131**.36
civic involvement, young people **131**.31-2
civil liberties
and media regulation **142**.1-2
civil marriage ceremonies **166**.6; **191**.3
civil partnerships **153**.26-30
dissolution **166**.21-2
numbers **153**.29-30
and parental responsibility **153**.33
Civil Partnerships Act **153**.26-8
civil rights on surveillance **168**.10
CJD (Creutzfeld Jacob disease) **141**.7
class *see* social class
class A drugs
young people's use **163**.26-7
class sizes (schools) **139**.1, 12
classification
of drugs **163**.2, 31, 33-4, 37; **186**.32-3
   effect on policing **186**.36-7
   reclassification of cannabis **163**.32, 35-6; **186**.4-5,
     31, 32
of films **196**.13-16
of video games **196**.17
Clean Development Mechanism **151**.21-2, 17

cleaner fuels **119**.20-23
Clearfield CL131 rice **138**.20
clearing (university entrance) **139**.30
climate change **193**.5
    benefits **151**.6
    and biodiversity **146**.19, 21
    and British tourism **156**.28
    Climate Change Bill **151**.17
    Climate Change Programme **146**.8
    and consumerism **134**.31
    controversies **151**.3-6
    denial of **151**.12-13, 14-15
    effects of **151**.1, 6, 8, 9, 10
    and food production **140**.17, 37
    and forests **146**.30
    and Galapagos Islands **193**.24-5
    and globalisation **157**.10
    hypocrisy about **151**.12-13
    and inequality **151**.11, 19
    and meat production **140**.17
    natural **151**.3
    and nuclear power **97**.19-20, 21, 22
    political action **151**.16-17, 27
    and population control **151**.31-2
    public action **151**. 38-9
    public awareness of factors contributing to **97**.34
    and renewable energy sources
        bioenergy **97**.18
        case for **97**.1-2
        and wind energy **97**.15
    and tourism **156**.1, 25
    tourist attitudes to **156**.28-30
    and transport emissions **119**.14, 30
    and whales and dolphins **193**.29
climate models **151**.5
clinical (major) depression **190**.2, 21
cloning
    animals **144**.30-39
    definition **144**.1, 4, 5, 18
    ethical issues **144**.2-3, 5-6, 7-8
    and factory farming **144**.35
    and food production **144**.36-9

    how it works **144**.1, 4, 14
    human **144**.1-14
    natural **144**.1
    regulations **144**.3
    risks **144**.2, 3, 6, 8
clostridium difficile **187**.28, 29
clothes
    as economic indicator **180**.5
    recycling **161**.28
clubs and societies at university **185**.6-7
CO_2 *see* carbon dioxide
co-parenting, same-sex couples **178**.9
coach travel, disabled people **197**.12
coal
    and carbon allowances **151**.37
    as an energy source **97**.4
coastal areas, effect of climate change **151**.10
cocaine **163**.4
    street sales **163**.12
    use prevalence **163**.7, 25
    worldwide production **163**.25
coffee growers and fairtrade **157**.32, 33
cognitive ability and gender **154**.24
Cognitive Behavioural Therapy (CBT) **141**.35
    and bipolar disorder **141**.14-15
    and eating disorders **184**.37-8
cognitive therapy for depression **190**.34
cohabitation **166**.1, 12, 14-15
    and expectation of marriage **166**.2, 7
    legal rights **166**.12, 14-15
collagen, stem cell therapy **144**.21-2
coming out **153**.3, 8
commercial sexual exploitation of children **156**.38-9
commercialisation, effect on children **134**.11-12
commodification of children **178**.12
'common law' marriages **166**.12
communication
    needs of disabled children **197**.37
    trends **158**.4-6
Communications Act and media mergers **142**.4
communications data **168**.8, 13-14, 32-3
    government database **168**.13-14

Volume numbers appear first (in bold) followed by page numbers; a change in volume number is preceded by a semi-**colon.**

Vol. 88 Food and Nutrition
Vol. 97 Energy Matters
Vol. 99 Exploited Children
Vol. 100 Stress and Anxiety
Vol. 119 Transport Trends
Vol. 129 Gambling Trends
Vol. 134 Customers and Consumerism
Vol. 138 A Genetically Modified Future?
Vol. 139 The Education Problem
Vol. 140 Vegetarian and Vegan Diets
Vol. 141 Mental Health
Vol. 142 Media Issues
Vol. 144 The Cloning Debate
Vol. 146 Sustainability and Environment
Vol. 147 The Terrorism Problem
Vol. 148 Religious Beliefs
Vol. 149 A Classless Society?
Vol. 150 Migration and Population
Vol. 151 Climate Change
Vol. 152 Euthanasia and the Right to Die
Vol. 153 Sexual Orientation and Society
Vol. 154 The Gender Gap
Vol. 155 Domestic Abuse

Vol. 156 Travel and Tourism
Vol. 157 The Problem of Globalisation
Vol. 158 The Internet Revolution
Vol. 159 An Ageing Population
Vol. 160 Poverty and Exclusion
Vol. 161 Waste Issues
Vol. 162 Staying Fit
Vol. 163 Drugs in the UK
Vol. 164 The AIDS Crisis
Vol. 165 Bullying Issues
Vol. 166 Marriage and Cohabitation
Vol. 167 Our Human Rights
Vol. 168 Privacy and Surveillance
Vol. 169 The Animal Rights Debate
Vol. 170 Body Image and Self-Esteem
Vol. 171 Abortion – Rights and Ethics
Vol. 172 Racial and Ethnic Discrimination
Vol. 173 Sexual Health
Vol. 174 Selling Sex
Vol. 175 Citizenship and Participation
Vol. 176 Health Issues for Young People
Vol. 177 Crime in the UK
Vol. 178 Reproductive Ethics

Vol. 179 Tackling Child Abuse
Vol. 180 Money and Finances
Vol. 181 The Housing Issue
Vol. 182 Teenage Conceptions
Vol. 183 Work and Employment
Vol. 184 Understanding Eating Disorders
Vol. 185 Student Matters
Vol. 186 Cannabis Use
Vol. 187 Health and the State
Vol. 188 Tobacco and Health
Vol. 189 The Homeless Population
Vol. 190 Coping with Depression
Vol. 191 The Changing Family
Vol. 192 Bereavement and Grief
Vol. 193 Endangered Species
Vol. 194 Responsible Drinking
Vol. 195 Alternative Medicine
Vol. 196 Censorship Issues
Vol. 197 Living with Disability
Vol. 198 Sport and Society
Vol. 199 Self-Harming and Suicide

privacy **168**.2
community arts **141**.38
community cohesion **131**.2
community disclosure of sex offenders **179**.20-21
community involvement, young people **131**.32
community sentences **177**.17, 24, 25-6, 27-9
    community orders **177**.24, 25-6
    community punishment orders **177**.17
    community rehabilitation orders **177**.17
    and knife crime **177**.38
compensation for faulty goods **134**.2, 17
compensation orders **177**.17, 25
competition
    and consumer choice **134**.1
    telecommunications industry **158**.6
competition scams **134**.26
competitive sport in schools **198**.5
complaints
    about goods **134**.2, 17
complementary and alternative medicine (CAM) **195**.1-13
    arguments against **195**.14-15
    definitions **195**.1, 9
    and depression **190**.11
    how it works **195**.2
    need for research **195**.13
    popularity **195**.3
    positive effects **195**.6-7
    reasons for using **195**.5, 6-7
    safety **195**.2
    therapists **195**.1, 3
    types **195**.3
    see also herbal medicine; homeopathy
complex carbohydrates **88**.2
complicated bereavement **192**.16-17
composting waste **161**.19, 28-9, 30
compulsions (obsessional rituals) **141**.17
compulsive eating **184**.7
compulsive exercise **162**.39; **184**.7
compulsive gambling **129**.2, 27-39
    causes **129**.29
    definition **129**.11
    drug treatment **129**.39
    and Gambling Commission **129**.5
    help for **129**.5, 29, 36, 37, 39
    online gambling **129**.21-2
    signs **129**.28, 29, 35-6, 38
    support groups **129**.37
    under 16s **129**.13, 25, 32-3
    women **129**.34
compulsive over-eating **184**.7
compulsive shopping **134**.13, 14
compulsory turnout to vote **131**.20-21
computers
    and euthanasia decision-making **152**.38-9
    home computer ownership **134**.5
    network attacks **196**.34
    recycling **161**.29
    spyware as tool of domestic abuse **155**.15-16
conception **178**.2-3; **182**.3-4
    rate, young people **173**.3; **182**.3
conciliation (mediation) **166**.26, 35, 38-9

condoms **173**.2, 24; **176**.27; **182**.19, 20
    and HIV **164**.3
    and the prevention of STIs **173**.24
    safe use **173**.5, 26
    usage **164**.26; **173**.22
confidence **170**.1, 8-9
congenital adrenal hyperplasia **154**.1
congestion, traffic **119**.11
    congestion charging **119**.12, 34-5, 38
    rail **119**.35
    and road building **119**.12
Congo, logging industry and wildlife **193**.4
conservation
    English environment **146**.32-3
    see also endangered species; extinction
Conservative party
    and GM crops **138**.39
constitutional change, impact on national identity **131**.5, 6
construction industry
    and energy efficiency **97**.36
    sustainability **146**.11
    waste recycling **161**.23
consultancies, tourism **156**.9
consumer adultery **161**.8-9
consumer assurance **134**.33-4
consumer choice **134**.1
consumer credit debt **134**.4, 23
consumer durables **134**.3-4, 5
consumer organisations **134**.21
consumer rights **134**.1-2, 17-21
    faulty goods **134**.2, 17
    and guarantees **134**.18-19
    private sales and auctions **134**.20
    and safety **134**.2
    second-hand goods **134**.20
consumer spending **134**.3-4
consumerism
    and body image **170**.30-31
    green consumerism **146**.38-9
    and mental health problems **134**.5
consumers **134**.1
    and animal welfare **140**.31, 33
    and child labour **99**.12
    disability discrimination **197**.21, 25
    ethical behaviour **134**.33-5
    and genetic modification **138**.9
    older people **159**.19
    rights *see* consumer rights
    satisfaction **134**.6
    spending *see* consumer spending
consumption
    global **193**.3-4
    sustainable **146**.7
    UK **150**.32
contact with children after divorce **166**.26, 37-8
contained (indoor) GMOs **138**.12
contamination
    groundwater **146**.36
    land **146**.22
    see also pollution
content sharing sites **142**.35

contraception **173**.1, 3, 5, 25; **176**.27; **182**.3-4, 19-26
    failure **173**.5
    and young people **173**.9; **182**.1-2
    see also condoms; family planning; pill, contraceptive
control orders **147**.3
copycat suicides and media reporting **199**.36
copyright
    and downloading **158**.35, 36
    and Freedom of Information Act **142**.19
coral reefs **193**.5
    economic value **193**.10
coronary heart disease (CHD) *see* heart disease
coroner **192**.31
corporal punishment **167**.36-9; **179**.30-38
    arguments against **179**.34-7
    arguments for not criminalising **179**.33
    and children's rights **167**.36-8; **179**.30, 31-2
    definition **179**.30, 34
    and discipline **179**.37
    effects **179**.34
    government position **179**.33
    and the law **179**.30
    public opposition to **179**.32
    and religious views **179**.36
cosmetic surgery **170**.32-6
    reasons for **170**.35
    statistics **170**.34-5, 36
    and stem cell therapy **144**.24-5
    teenagers **170**.32-3, 36
cosmic rays and climate change **151**.6
cost of living **180**.6
costs
    academies **139**.15
    of ageing **159**.19-30
    of alcohol **194**.35
        minimum pricing **194**.36, 37
    of alien invasive species **193**.12
    of cannabis **186**.2
    of child poverty **160**.11
    of civil partnerships **153**.28
    of cleaner vehicles **119**.20-24
    of dementia **159**.35
    of domestic violence **155**.25
    of education **139**.1, 35; **160**.16-17, 19
    of fly-tipping **161**.16
    of free range food production **169**.11-12
    fuel **160**.22-3
    of funerals **192**.30-31
    of global warming **151**.8
    of higher education **185**.11, 17
    home buying **181**.24
    home care for the elderly **159**.26
    identity cards **131**.13; **168**.17, 18-19
    of identity theft **168**.39
    motoring **119**.14
    private health care **187**.24
    smoking **188**.15, 22-3
    of social exclusion **149**.39
    of student life **185**.11
    university degrees **139**.35; **185**.11, 17
    of vegan diet **140**.25
    of wasted food **161**.10-11
    of work-related stress **183**.6-7
    of workplace bullying **165**.39
    of zero emission fuels **151**.28-9
cotinine and passive smoking **188**.12
cotton
    fairtrade **157**.28, 34
    genetically modified **138**.35
council tax
    and civil partnerships **153**.28
    and young people **181**.26
council tenants
    and right to move **181**.35-6
    rights **181**.16
    see also social housing
councils *see* local authorities
counselling **141**.35
    after abortion **171**.5
    for depression **190**.34
    and help with stress **100**.32, 34
    and testing for HIV **96**.1
counter-terrorism **147**.2, 26-39
    and online activities **147**.9

Volume numbers appear first (in bold) followed by page numbers; a change in volume number is preceded by a semi-**colon**.

Vol. 88 Food and Nutrition
Vol. 97 Energy Matters
Vol. 99 Exploited Children
Vol. 100 Stress and Anxiety
Vol. 119 Transport Trends
Vol. 129 Gambling Trends
Vol. 134 Customers and Consumerism
Vol. 138 A Genetically Modified Future?
Vol. 139 The Education Problem
Vol. 140 Vegetarian and Vegan Diets
Vol. 141 Mental Health
Vol. 142 Media Issues
Vol. 144 The Cloning Debate
Vol. 146 Sustainability and Environment
Vol. 147 The Terrorism Problem
Vol. 148 Religious Beliefs
Vol. 149 A Classless Society?
Vol. 150 Migration and Population
Vol. 151 Climate Change
Vol. 152 Euthanasia and the Right to Die
Vol. 153 Sexual Orientation and Society
Vol. 154 The Gender Gap
Vol. 155 Domestic Abuse

Vol. 156 Travel and Tourism
Vol. 157 The Problem of Globalisation
Vol. 158 The Internet Revolution
Vol. 159 An Ageing Population
Vol. 160 Poverty and Exclusion
Vol. 161 Waste Issues
Vol. 162 Staying Fit
Vol. 163 Drugs in the UK
Vol. 164 The AIDS Crisis
Vol. 165 Bullying Issues
Vol. 166 Marriage and Cohabitation
Vol. 167 Our Human Rights
Vol. 168 Privacy and Surveillance
Vol. 169 The Animal Rights Debate
Vol. 170 Body Image and Self-Esteem
Vol. 171 Abortion – Rights and Ethics
Vol. 172 Racial and Ethnic Discrimination
Vol. 173 Sexual Health
Vol. 174 Selling Sex
Vol. 175 Citizenship and Participation
Vol. 176 Health Issues for Young People
Vol. 177 Crime in the UK
Vol. 178 Reproductive Ethics

Vol. 179 Tackling Child Abuse
Vol. 180 Money and Finances
Vol. 181 The Housing Issue
Vol. 182 Teenage Conceptions
Vol. 183 Work and Employment
Vol. 184 Understanding Eating Disorders
Vol. 185 Student Matters
Vol. 186 Cannabis Use
Vol. 187 Health and the State
Vol. 188 Tobacco and Health
Vol. 189 The Homeless Population
Vol. 190 Coping with Depression
Vol. 191 The Changing Family
Vol. 192 Bereavement and Grief
Vol. 193 Endangered Species
Vol. 194 Responsible Drinking
Vol. 195 Alternative Medicine
Vol. 196 Censorship Issues
Vol. 197 Living with Disability
Vol. 198 Sport and Society
Vol. 199 Self-Harming and Suicide

targeting terrorist funds **147**.3, 28-9
UK strategy **147**.28-9
countryside
    affordable housing **181**.3
    and the Hunting Act **169**.31-2
    and the production and use of energy **97**.24-5
coursework and Internet plagiarism **158**.19-20
courts of law
    divorce process **166**.36
    and torture evidence **167**.27
crabs (pubic lice) **173**.17-18
crack cocaine **163**.4
creationism **148**.37
    teaching 36
creativity, and mental health **141**.38
credit **180**.26-7
    consumer credit levels **134**.4, 23, 24
    credit purchases **180**.27
    types of **134**.22; **180**.26-7
    unrequested **180**.15
    using wisely **134**.22
    see also debt
credit cards **134**.22, 24; **180**.14, 26
    and consumer rights **134**.18
    international usage, women **180**.19
    limits, unrequested increases **180**.15
    store cards **180**.14, 26
credit crunch **180**.2-3, 4
    see also recession
crime **177**.1-39
    and alcohol **176**.15; **194**.20, 21, 29
    controlling movement of criminals in EU **150**.7
    costs of **149**.39
    cybercrime **158**.35
    and domestic violence **155**.2
    and drugs **163**.2-3, 23
    and educational underachievement **149**.39
    fear of **159**.3; **177**.2, 6, 20-21
    filesharing **158**.36
    and forced marriages **155**.17
    HIV transmission as crime **164**.12-14
    identity theft **158**.3
    levels of crime **177**.20
    and licensing hours change **194**.21
    and migrants **150**.12, 13, 14
    and mobile phones **158**.12-13
    phishing **158**.36
    public worry about **177**.2, 6, 20-21
    racially motivated **115**.9-10
    religiously motivated **115**.27; **148**.29
    and surveillance **168**.27
    victims of see victims of crime
    Wi-Fi hijacking **158**.37
    youth crime, costs of **149**.39
crime prevention and CCTV **168**.23-4
criminal justice system
    and domestic violence **155**.35-8
    and gender equality **154**.4
    youth courts **177**.16-18
criminal responsibility, age of **177**.19
crocodile farming **140**.30

crop biotechnology see genetically modified (GM) crops
crop rotation **88**.14
cross-contamination, genetic **138**.4
cross-cultural communication **142**.34
cross-pollination, GM and non-GM crops **138**.6-7, 12-13
cryogenic ID tags and IVF **178**.22-3
cryopreservation see freezing
crystal meth (methamphetamine) **163**.16-17, 32
cultural capital **149**.2
cultural Christianity **148**.23-5
cultural differences and mixed-faith relationships **115**.39
cultural traditions
    British **131**.1
    and death **192**.29, 34-6
culture
    and biological environment **146**.19
    and body image **170**.20
    and corporal punishment **179**.36
    and domestic violence **155**.4
    and fatherhood **191**.33
    and gender discrimination **154**.13-14
    and health inequalities **149**.14
    and the media **142**.34
    and religion **148**.23-5
    effect of tourism **156**.22
curfew orders **177**.17, 25
current accounts **180**.25
custody see prison; youth custody
customs, drugs seizures **163**.37
customs regulations, indecent articles **196**.23
cutting (self-harm)
    emergency treatment **199**.13-14
    safety measures **199**.7
cyanovirin-N **138**.22
cyber safety **165**.26-7, 30-31
cyberbullying **165**.2, 9, 23-31
    anti-bullying strategies **165**.25-6
    definitions **165**.23, 25
    extent of **165**.28, 29
    and the law **165**.25
    preventing **165**.25-6
    responding to **165**.26
    at work **165**.37-9
cybercrime **158**.35
cyberterrorism **147**.8-9
cybrids (animal-human hybrids) **144**.9, 10-12
cycling **119**.25, 29
    children **119**.28
    health benefits **119**.39
    helmets **119**.28
    to school **119**.30
cyclothymia **190**.9
cystic fibrosis research, animal experimentation **144**.34

D

D&E (surgical dilation and evacuation) **171**.3
DAB digital radio **158**.5
dairy foods **88**.6, 15
dairy-free diet **140**.22-3, 26

dark tourism **156**.35-6

data protection

  personal protection measures **168**.31-2, 37

  and self-regulation **168**.2

Data Protection Act **168**.10-11, 31, 37

date rape drugs **194**.8-10

daylight, effect on mental health **141**.35

death sites as tourist venues **156**.35-6

death tourism **152**.16

deaths

  after abortion **171**.6, 12

  alcohol-related **194**.13

  of children **192**.20-23

    cyclists **119**.28

    pedestrians **119**.5, 30

  children's understanding of death **192**.4, 13, 15, 19

  discussing own wishes about dying **192**.8, 24

  and drug misuse **163**.11-12

  funerals **192**.30-31, 34-7

  older people, winter **159**.4

  practical matters **192**.24, 29-33

  registering **192**.29-30

  in road accidents **119**.4, 5, 30

  see also bereavement

debauchery tourism **156**.36

debit cards **134**.24; **180**.13, 26

debt **134**.23-5; **160**.32-3; **180**.9-12

  advice **134**.23, 25; **180**.27

  affecting more affluent people **180**.10

  buying on credit **134**.22

  debt bondage **167**.22

  developing world **157**.5, 9-10; **160**.33

  icreasing incidence of debt **180**.11

  need for education about debt **180**.38

  and poverty **160**.12

  and social class **149**.20

  statistics **134**.4, 23, 24; **180**.9, 10, 11, 12

  students **134**.24; **185**.12-13, 17

  and young people **134**.24

debt crisis **157**.5; **180**.10-12

decision-making

  in euthanasia cases **152**.38-9

young people **131**.28

  feelings of exclusion **131**.26

decontamination of land, by plants **138**.14

decree absolute **166**.22, 26

decree nisi **166**.22, 26

deer, as food **140**.15, 17

default retirement age **183**.14-15

defensive verbalisation **170**.13

deferred sentences **177**.18

deforestation **146**.30-31

  and cattle ranching **193**.14

  and palm oil industry **193**.14

degrees, university

  costs **139**.34, 35; **185**.11, 17

  courses **139**.2, 29, 30, 38-9; **185**.5-6

  and earnings **139**.35, 36, 37; **185**.21, 32-4

  and ethnicity **139**.8

  and gender **139**.10

  for nurses **187**.33-5

  results rising **139**.33

dementia **141**.6-8; **159**.4, 35-9

  fear of **159**.39

  see also Alzheimer's disease

democracy

  and extremism **131**.23-4

  proposal for reform **131**.25

  see also elections

demonstrations

  by Muslim extremists against British soldiers **196**.9, 10

  via the Internet **196**.32

Denmark

  cartoons of Muhammed **142**.34

  state pension **159**.25

dental dams **96**.2

dependency **141**.9-10

  on alcohol **194**.6, 15

depersonalisation **141**.11

depressant drugs (downers) **163**.2, 5-6

depression **190**.1-39

  and body image **170**.19

  and cannabis use **186**.10

  causes of **190**.2-3, 4, 5

Volume numbers appear first (in bold) followed by page numbers; a change in volume number is preceded by a semi-**colon.**

Vol. 88 Food and Nutrition

Vol. 97 Energy Matters

Vol. 99 Exploited Children

Vol. 100 Stress and Anxiety

Vol. 119 Transport Trends

Vol. 129 Gambling Trends

Vol. 134 Customers and Consumerism

Vol. 138 A Genetically Modified Future?

Vol. 139 The Education Problem

Vol. 140 Vegetarian and Vegan Diets

Vol. 141 Mental Health

Vol. 142 Media Issues

Vol. 144 The Cloning Debate

Vol. 146 Sustainability and Environment

Vol. 147 The Terrorism Problem

Vol. 148 Religious Beliefs

Vol. 149 A Classless Society?

Vol. 150 Migration and Population

Vol. 151 Climate Change

Vol. 152 Euthanasia and the Right to Die

Vol. 153 Sexual Orientation and Society

Vol. 154 The Gender Gap

Vol. 155 Domestic Abuse

Vol. 156 Travel and Tourism

Vol. 157 The Problem of Globalisation

Vol. 158 The Internet Revolution

Vol. 159 An Ageing Population

Vol. 160 Poverty and Exclusion

Vol. 161 Waste Issues

Vol. 162 Staying Fit

Vol. 163 Drugs in the UK

Vol. 164 The AIDS Crisis

Vol. 165 Bullying Issues

Vol. 166 Marriage and Cohabitation

Vol. 167 Our Human Rights

Vol. 168 Privacy and Surveillance

Vol. 169 The Animal Rights Debate

Vol. 170 Body Image and Self-Esteem

Vol. 171 Abortion – Rights and Ethics

Vol. 172 Racial and Ethnic Discrimination

Vol. 173 Sexual Health

Vol. 174 Selling Sex

Vol. 175 Citizenship and Participation

Vol. 176 Health Issues for Young People

Vol. 177 Crime in the UK

Vol. 178 Reproductive Ethics

Vol. 179 Tackling Child Abuse

Vol. 180 Money and Finances

Vol. 181 The Housing Issue

Vol. 182 Teenage Conceptions

Vol. 183 Work and Employment

Vol. 184 Understanding Eating Disorders

Vol. 185 Student Matters

Vol. 186 Cannabis Use

Vol. 187 Health and the State

Vol. 188 Tobacco and Health

Vol. 189 The Homeless Population

Vol. 190 Coping with Depression

Vol. 191 The Changing Family

Vol. 192 Bereavement and Grief

Vol. 193 Endangered Species

Vol. 194 Responsible Drinking

Vol. 195 Alternative Medicine

Vol. 196 Censorship Issues

Vol. 197 Living with Disability

Vol. 198 Sport and Society

Vol. 199 Self-Harming and Suicide

in children and young people **176**.30, 32

and complementary therapies **190**.11

definitions **190**.21-2

and desire for success **190**.13

diagnosis

    bipolar disorder **190**.8

    GPs difficulty diagnosing depression **190**.31

    teenage depression **190**.25-6

and exam stress **100**.7

and exercise **141**.39; **162**.37, 38, **190**.3, 38

genetic factors **190**.2, 4, 11, 12-13

and incapacity benefit **100**.23

manic depression *see* bipolar affective disorder

and meditation **195**.15

and men **190**.18-19

and mortality **190**.20

and physical illness **190**.3, 5

post-natal **190**.2, 14-17, 21-2

prevalence of **141**.1, 2; **190**.22-3, 30

and redundancy **183**.11

statistics **190**.7, 27, 30

and stress **100**.1, 24

students **185**.8

and suicide **190**.21, 23-4

    young people **190**.26-7

symptoms **190**.1-2; 21, 22; **199**.29

    bipolar disorder **190**.8-9, 21

    post-natal depression **190**.14

    seasonal affective disorder **190**.6

    young people **190**.26

treatments **190**.31-9

    young people **190**.25

    drugs **190**.10-11, 26, 32-3

    manic depression **190**.10-11

    psychotherapy **190**.5, 11, 34, 37

    Seasonal Affective Disorder **190**.6-7

    self-help **190**.38-9

types of **190**.2, 21-2

unipolar (endogenous) **190**.10

young people **176**.30, 32; **190**.25-30

    and university **176**.6

deprived areas as tourist sights **156**.33-5

derealisation **141**.11

desertification

    causing migration **146**.16

designer babies **178**.31-2

designer holidays **156**.2

detention and training orders **177**.17-18

developing countries

    abortions **171**.11-12

    ageing populations **159**.5

    aid to *see* aid

    and AIDS/HIV **96**.17-18, 36-7; **164**.10

    child labour in **99**.1, 2

    and climate change action **151**.19

    damaging effects of recycling **161**.35

    debt and poverty **157**.9-10

    effect of EU GM controls **138**.29-30

    and free trade **157**.20, 25, 26-7

    and gap years **156**.15-19

    and globalisation **157**.25

and GM crops **138**.9, 10, 23, 34-5

and homeopathy, WHO warnings **195**.30-31

money deposits in UK **146**.6

pensions **159**.24

receiving unwanted waste **161**.37

and tourism

    problems **156**.22

    slum tours **156**.33-5

    sustainable tourism **156**.22-3

    tourism dependency **156**.21

and World Trade Organization **157**.22, 24

development

    effect on environment **146**.24

    and migration **150**.2

development aid, contributing to climate change **151**.27

devolution, effect on national identity **131**.5, 6

diet

    and Buddhism **148**. 11

    and Christianity **148**.2, 10

    healthy *see* healthy eating

    and Hinduism **148**.3, 11

    and Islam **148**.3-4, 11

    and Judaism **148**.4, 10-11

    macrobiotic **195**.4-5

    and mental health **141**.30-31, 34; **190**.3

    and religion **148**.10-11

    and Sikhism **148**.5

    and stress **100**.19, 30, 31, 35

    and weight loss **162**.2

    worldwide changes **162**.6

    young people **176**.8-9

diet industry and body image **170**.31

dietary obsession (orthorexia nervosa) **184**.9

dieting

    mothers, effects on daughters **184**.21-2

    teenage girls **184**.22

digital entertainment **158**.3, 5, 7, 21-2

digital radio **158**.5

digital television **158**.5

Dignitas **152**.30

dignity *see* human dignity

direct debits **180**.14

direct discrimination **153**.37-8

direct mail scams **134**.26-8

direct racial discrimination **115**.7, 11

disability

    and abortion **171**.22

    acceptable language **197**.27

    benefits **197**.31-4

    and bullying **165**.9, 14-17

    definitions **197**.1-2

    discrimination **197**.20-23

        in healthcare **197**.30-31, 38-9

        workplace **197**.20-21

    and employment **197**.20-21, 24-5, 26-7

    hidden disabilities **197**.8

    learning disabilities **197**.6-7

    physical disabilities **197**.3-5

    and poverty **160**.10, 25; **197**.35

    and transport **197**.11-12, 23

Disability Discrimination Act **197**.8-9, 24-5

and workplace stress **100**.17, 20, 22

Disability Living Allowance **197**.31-4

disability rights
    access to goods and services **197**.21, 25
    education **197**.22-3
    housing **197**.21-2
    transport **197**.11-12, 23
    at work **197**.20-21, 24-5, 26-7

disabled children
    learning disabilities **197**.14-15
    needs **197**.36-7
    physical disabilities **197**.3-5
    siblings of disabled children **197**.18-19

disabled people
    and assisted suicide **152**.20-21; **199**.39
    bullying of **165**.9, 14-17
    discrimination **197**.20-23, 30-31, 38-9
    and employment **197**.20-21, 24-5, 26-7
    model used in advertising campaign **197**.10
    and sport **198**.18, 20-21
    and transport **197**.11-12, 23

disablism *see* discrimination, disabled people

disaster victims, older people **159**.6

discharges (criminal) **177**.17, 24-5

discipline
    role of fathers **191**.31-2
    see also corporal punishment; smacking

discretionary eviction **181**.16

discrimination
    anti-discrimination legislation **183**.13
    and child labour **99**.4
    direct and indirect **115**.7, 11
    disabled people **197**.20-23
      in healthcare **197**.30-31, 38-9
      at work **197**.20-21
    against middle class university applications **149**.7
    and obesity **162**.21
    racial *see* racial discrimination
    sexual orientation **153**.2-3
      in employment **153**.37-8
    by social class **149**.2
    in the workplace **153**.37-8; **197**.20-21

disease
    Millennium Development Goals **160**.32
    water-related **146**.14, 15

disposable nappies, waste **161**.1, 5, 29

dissociative disorders **141**.11-13

distraction techniques, self-harmers **199**.5-6, 8

diuretics as banned substances in sport **198**.29

diversity, Britain **156**.11

divorce **166**.3, 21-39
    and children **166**.4-5, 29-31, 32, 34-8; **191**.1, 9
    and duration of marriage **166**.27, 28
    emotional effects **166**.22-4
    how to help **166**.24
    legal process **166**.22
    reasons for **166**.21-2
    risk factors **166**.28
    statistics **166**.3, 4, 6, 25, 27, 28; **191**.1, 8

DIY abortions **171**.35-6

DNA **138**.4, 12; **144**.17; **168**.7, 11-12
    damage by cannabis use **186**.14

DNA database **177**.31-2

doctors
    and abortion **171**.25-8
    asking about patient's alcohol consumption **194**.33, 37-8
    and euthanasia **152**.7, 8, 24-6, 27-8
    fears of rise in gambling **129**.31
    GP patient survey **187**.16-17
    and help for eating disorders **184**.36
    relationship with patients **187**.31
    role in NHS **187**.25, 26
    trusted by the public **187**.18

doctrine of double effect **152**.1, 3, 5

Dolly the sheep **144**.1, 15, 30-31, 32, 34, 39

dolphins, impact of climate change **193**.29

domestic abuse **155**.1-39
    children **189**.27
    convictions **155**.36-7
    definitions **155**.1, 27
    help for perpetrators **155**.33-4
    helplines **155**.28-9
    impact on children **155**.1, 4, 5, 19-25

Volume numbers appear first (in bold) followed by page numbers; a change in volume number is preceded by a semi-**colon.**

Vol. 88 Food and Nutrition
Vol. 97 Energy Matters
Vol. 99 Exploited Children
Vol. 100 Stress and Anxiety
Vol. 119 Transport Trends
Vol. 129 Gambling Trends
Vol. 134 Customers and Consumerism
Vol. 138 A Genetically Modified Future?
Vol. 139 The Education Problem
Vol. 140 Vegetarian and Vegan Diets
Vol. 141 Mental Health
Vol. 142 Media Issues
Vol. 144 The Cloning Debate
Vol. 146 Sustainability and Environment
Vol. 147 The Terrorism Problem
Vol. 148 Religious Beliefs
Vol. 149 A Classless Society?
Vol. 150 Migration and Population
Vol. 151 Climate Change
Vol. 152 Euthanasia and the Right to Die
Vol. 153 Sexual Orientation and Society
Vol. 154 The Gender Gap
Vol. 155 Domestic Abuse

Vol. 156 Travel and Tourism
Vol. 157 The Problem of Globalisation
Vol. 158 The Internet Revolution
Vol. 159 An Ageing Population
Vol. 160 Poverty and Exclusion
Vol. 161 Waste Issues
Vol. 162 Staying Fit
Vol. 163 Drugs in the UK
Vol. 164 The AIDS Crisis
Vol. 165 Bullying Issues
Vol. 166 Marriage and Cohabitation
Vol. 167 Our Human Rights
Vol. 168 Privacy and Surveillance
Vol. 169 The Animal Rights Debate
Vol. 170 Body Image and Self-Esteem
Vol. 171 Abortion – Rights and Ethics
Vol. 172 Racial and Ethnic Discrimination
Vol. 173 Sexual Health
Vol. 174 Selling Sex
Vol. 175 Citizenship and Participation
Vol. 176 Health Issues for Young People
Vol. 177 Crime in the UK
Vol. 178 Reproductive Ethics

Vol. 179 Tackling Child Abuse
Vol. 180 Money and Finances
Vol. 181 The Housing Issue
Vol. 182 Teenage Conceptions
Vol. 183 Work and Employment
Vol. 184 Understanding Eating Disorders
Vol. 185 Student Matters
Vol. 186 Cannabis Use
Vol. 187 Health and the State
Vol. 188 Tobacco and Health
Vol. 189 The Homeless Population
Vol. 190 Coping with Depression
Vol. 191 The Changing Family
Vol. 192 Bereavement and Grief
Vol. 193 Endangered Species
Vol. 194 Responsible Drinking
Vol. 195 Alternative Medicine
Vol. 196 Censorship Issues
Vol. 197 Living with Disability
Vol. 198 Sport and Society
Vol. 199 Self-Harming and Suicide

injuries sustained **155**.30
leaving home **155**.4-5, 6-7, 12-13, 27-8
legal protection **155**.28
male victims **155**.12-13
myths and stereotypes **155**.3-5
personal stories **155**.8-10, 22-4
prevalence of **154**.12; **155**.5,10
register of offenders **155**.39
reluctance to seek help **155**.3-4, 5, 6, 7, 30-31
same-sex relationships **155**.13-15
seeking help **155**.3-4, 7, 30-31
signs of abuse **155**.1-2
statistics **155**.24-5
support for victims **155**.6-7, 28-9
tackling abuse **155**.27-39
and young people **155**.21, 26
domestic appliances, household ownership **134**.3-4, 5
domestic violence and teenagers **179**.19
domestic waste *see* household waste
domestic workers
    children as **99**.1, 4, 7-10; **167**.32
    migrant workers **150**.15
    slavery **167**.22, 32
donor insemination **178**.9
donors, eggs and sperm
    contact with offspring **178**.25, 26-7
    donor anonymity **178**.11, 24
    numbers falling **178**.24
    and parental rights **153**.34
doomsday tourism **156**.27
doorstep selling and consumer rights **134**.20
dopamine **141**.9
doping *see* drugs in sport
Down's syndrome
    and Alzheimer's disease **141**.7
downers *see* depressant drugs
downloading **158**.35-6
downshifting **183**.18
drag hunting **169**.33
dress code
    Christianty **148**.2
    Hinduism **148**.3
    Islam **148**.4
    Judaism **148**.4
    Sikhism **148**.5
drink-driving **119**.8-9; **194**.31
    reducing alcohol limit **194**.32
drink spiking **194**.8-10
driver behaviour **119**.7-9
driving
    and alcohol *see* drink-driving
    and cannabis use **186**.10
    and disabled people **197**.11
    driving licences, EU **168**.9
    and mobile phones **158**.12
drug abuse **163**.1, 3, 7; **176**.6, 19
    and abortion **171**.9
    and beggars **189**.35-6
    costs **163**.21
    deaths from **163**.11-12
    declining **163**.22

and fertility **178**.4, 5
frequency **163**.3
and HIV **96**.14, 26; **164**.17, 25
and homeless people **189**.10, 13, 35-6
and sex **173**.15
and smoking **176**.12
statistics **163**.3, 7, 24, 32; **176**.18
students **185**.8, 9
worldwide **163**.25; **186**.18-21
young people **163**.3, 15-16, 18-19, 26-30; **176**.6, 18
see also cannabis
drug addiction **163**.2
drug development
    and animal experiments *see* animal experiments
    use of stem cells **144**.18
drug misuse **163**.1
drug overdoses **163**.12
    emergency treatment **199**.14
drug rehabilitation orders for offenders **177**.18, 26
drug testing
    in sport **198**.27, 28
        punishment for missing tests **198**.39
    at work **168**.38
drug treatment and testing orders **177**.18
drug treatments
    for depression **190**.32-3
        for bipolar disorder 10-11
        as cause of depression **190**.3
        and teenage depression **190**.26
        see also anti-depressants
    for gambling **129**.39
drugs
    for abortion **171**.2, 35, 36
    assessment of drug harms **186**.33
    assessment for NHS use **187**.22-3
    buying pharmaceutical drugs **195**.8
    cannabis *see* cannabis
    classification **163**.2, 31, 33-4, 37
        cannabis **163**.32, 35-6; **186**.4-5, 31, 32-3
        criticism of **163**.32
    and crime **163**.2-3, 23, 38
    date rape drugs **194**.8-10
    definitions **163**.1, 31
    and dependency **141**.9
    effects
        amphetamines **163**.4-5
        cannabis **163**.6, 9, 35-6; **186**.1-29
        cocaine **163**.4
        ecstasy **163**.5, 9-10
        ketamine **163**.19-20
        LSD **163**.6
        magic mushrooms **163**.6
        opiates **163**.5
        solvents **163**.6
    and fertility **178**.4, 5
    global illicit drugs problem **186**.20-21
    government policies **186**.35-6
    and the law **163**.1-2, 31-9; **176**.19
    and obscenity law **196**.22
    patients' rights under NHS **187**.14
    and politics **163**.31-2; **186**.34-6

smuggling **163**.37-8

support for families of drug users **163**.24

types **163**.2

for weight loss **162**.2-3, 6, 20

and young people **163**.3, 9, 15-16; 18-19; 26-30

see also drug abuse

drugs in sport **198**.27-39

anabolic steroids **198**.29-30

analgesics **198**.28-9

arguments for and against **198**.33-7

dangers **198**.34

diuretics **198**.29

drug testing **198**.27, 28, 39

history of **198**.32

hormones **198**.29-30

reasons for taking drugs **198**.28, 32

stimulants **198**.29

therapeutic use exemption **198**.28

drunkorexia **184**.16

dual diagnosis, homeless people **189**.10-11

DVDs, recycling **161**.23

dysthymia **190**.10, 21, 23

E

e-cigarettes **188**.21

E.coli **187**.28

e-commerce, Europe **134**.15-16

e-learning **139**.28

e-mail

bullying **165**.23-4, 38-9

phishing **134**.27-8, 28-9

security measures **134**.28

surveillance of **168**.8

E-number food additives and vegetarianism **140**.18

early medical abortion (EMA) **171**.26

earnings

effect of education **139**.1

footballers **198**.11-12

gender gap *see* gender pay gap

graduates **139**.35, 36, 37; **183**.34; **185**.32-4

and social class **149**.2

and university status **185**.21

minimum wage, young workers **183**.28

teachers **139**.12

see also incomes; salaries; wages

ears, stem cell therapy **144**.22

eating disorders **176**.9, 30, 39; **184**.1-16

and body image **170**.19

causes **184**.2, 4, 5, 6, 28

and compulsive exercise **162**.39

effects **184**.1-2

getting help **184**.2, 29-39

risk factors **184**.2, 13

students **185**.8

teenagers **184**.21-2, 30-31

and going to university **176**.6

see also anorexia nervosa; bulimia nervosa; obesity

eco-lodges **156**.24

ecological debt **146**.4-6; **150**.32

ecological footprints **146**.10, 17

ecological overshoot **146**.10

economic globalisation **157**.2

economic growth

Britain **134**.24

costs of **157**.13

and globalisation **157**.36-7

and higher education **183**.34

impact of educational underachievement **149**.39

impact of immigration **150**.11, 17

indicators of recovery **180**.5

economy

global, and biodiversity **193**.10-12

recession **180**.1-5

and tobacco **188**.22-3

ecosystems

biodiversity **146**.18,19

and climate change **151**.9

ecotourism **156**.20, 24

eco-towns **151**.32; **181**.36-9

eco-travel spending **134**.32

ecstasy (MDMA) **163**.5, 9-10

deaths fron **163**.11

safety **163**.34
street sales **163**.12-13
use, Europe **163**.25
ECT (electro-convulsive therapy) **190**.11
ED-NOS (eating disorder not otherwise specified) **184**.7-8
education **139**.1-39
on abortion **171**.36-9
and alcohol **194**.20
and black history **115**.16-17
and black pupils **115**.19-21
and the Budget **180**.24
effects of cannabis use **186**.9-10
and child labour **99**.3, 7, 15; **167**.31
and child soldiers **99**.31
costs **139**.1; **160**.16-17
and disabled children **197**.14-15, 22-3, 37
on drugs **163**.24
and earnings **139**.1, 35, 36, 37
and ethnicity **139**.8-9
faith-based schools **148**.34, 35-6
and family income **149**.25
financial **180**.36-9
and gender **139**.10-11; **154**.12, 22-7
global gender inequality **154**.12
higher education **139**.29-39
    government funding **180**.28, 33
about HIV **164**.18, 23-4
home learning **139**.27-8
as a human right **167**.23
on intelligent design **148**.39
international comparisons **183**.34
and learning disabilities **197**.14-15
in mental health **141**.37
Millennium Development Goals **160**.30-31
and minority ethnic pupils **115**.18
multi-faith schools **148**.32-3
and parents' mental health problems **141**.24
and poverty **160**.2, 17-22
and racial integration **115**.29, 30, 37
and racism **115**.19-20
and social division **177**.4
and social mobility **139**.13; **149**.22, 25, 30, 36-7
special educational needs (SEN) **197**.14-15, 23
statistics **139**.1-2
teaching happiness **170**.14-15
and teenage pregnancy **182**.31
underachievement, costs of **149**.39
and war-affected children **99**.34
and young people with HIV/AIDS **96**.26, 32, 33
educational achievement
black pupils **115**.20
and ethnicity **139**.8
and family income **149**.25
gender differences **154**.22, 23
effect of poverty **160**.2, 18-19, 20, 21
and school pupil intake **149**.31-3
and single-sex schooling **139**.11-12
and social class **149**.30, 31-3
see also exam results
egg donation **178**.10-12
for embryonic stem cell research **178**.34-5

numbers declining **178**.24
risks **178**.12
egg freezing **178**.23
eggs
consumer choices **140**.37-8
free-range **140**.6, 29, 38-9
from GM hens, and cancer treatment **138**.20-21
and health **140**.30, 39
production methods **140**.29, 38-9
sales **140**.37-8
and vegetarian diets **140**.6, 19, 26
ejaculation **178**.3
disorders **178**.5
elderly people
and dementia see dementia
elder abuse **159**.4, 6, 16-18
and mental health problems **141**.2
and suicide **199**.20, 21
see also ageing population; grandparents; older people
elections **131**.16-22
campaigns **131**.18
European **131**.15
General Elections **131**.18
terminology **131**.17
voter turnout **131**.19-21
electoral register **131**.16
electoral system **131**.15-26
electric hybrid vehicles **119**.22
electric vehicles **119**.21-2
electro-convulsive therapy (ECT) **190**.11
electronic cigarettes **188**.21
electronic equipment recycling **161**.8-9, 23-4
electronic footprints **158**.10-11
elephants, as endangered species **193**.2, 19
ELVs, recycling **161**.23
embarkation controls **150**.7
embryo cloning see human reproductive cloning
embryo donation **144**.7
for research **178**.37
embryo freezing, effects on health **178**.22
embryo selection **178**.28-32
embryonic stem cell research **144**.2
Catholic Church opposition **178**.35
ethical issues **144**.6; **178**.33-5
humanist view **144**.7-8, **178**.36-7
embryos
hybrid **144**.9, 11, 14, 20; **178**.35
moral status **178**.33-4
emergency contraception **173**.5, 25; **176**.27; **182**.5
emergency treatment, self-harmers **199**.13-14
emigrants
British **150**.24-5
definition **150**.21
emissions
calculations **151**.22
reduction **151**.2, 13, 17, 36-7
transport **119**.1, 15, 31
aircraft **119**.16
and climate change **119**.14, 24, 30
emotional abuse **155**.3; **179**.1
signs of **179**.5

emotional changes, and stress **100**.33
emotional distress and self-harm **199**.2
emotional extremes and self-harm **199**.10-11
emotional health
    and homelessness **189**.9
    problems of consumerism **134**.5
    see also mental health
emotional impact
    of abortion **171**.5
    of divorce **166**.22-4
    of domestic violence **155**.30
    of poor body image **170**.19
    of redundancy **183**.11
emotional skills **170**.5
emotions, animals **140**.27-8; **169**.2-3
employees
    gambling at work **129**.22-4
    surveillance **168**.9. 27, 38
employers
    basic skills requirements **139**.17
    equality policies **115**.13
    liability for racism **115**.12
    links with higher education **139**.38-9
    workforce monitoring by GPS **168**.27
    workplace monitoring **168**.38
    and workplace stress **100**.17-18, 20
employment
    and age discrimination **159**.8-13
    barriers to **160**.13
    census information **150**.36
    difficulty finding jobs **180**.34-5
    Disability Symbol **197**.26-7
    of disabled people **197**.20-21, 24-5, 26-7
    as economic indicator **180**.5
    effect of free trade **157**.13, 23
    effects of recession **180**.3
    employment status and smoking **188**.2
    and gender **154**.29-35
    effect of globalisation **157**.36-7
    graduates **139**.33; **185**.30, 31-2, 36-7
        value of extra-curricula interests **185**.7
    and homelessness **189**.33

inequalities **149**.28
    and mental illness **141**.22
    effect of migration **150**.9-10
    and obesity discrimination **162**.21
    from recycling **161**.2
    past retirement age **159**.10, 15
    and racism **115**.12, 13
    rights
        awareness of **183**.10
        disability rights **197**.20-21, 24-5, 26-7
        maternity rights **191**.37-8
        parental leave **191**.34 39
        paternity rights **191**.34-5, 39
    sexual orientation discrimination **153**.37-9
    students **139**.35; **180**.29
    tourism industry **156**.10
    working conditions, international companies **157**.11
    young people and the law **180**.20
Employment Equality (Sexual Orientation) Regulations **153**.37
empty forest syndrome **193**.20
empty nest syndrome **191**.29
endangered species **193**.1-2
    butterflies **193**.36
    elephants **193**.19
    fish **193**.30
    invertebrates **193**.26
    pollinating insects **193**.27-8
    primates **193**.22-3
    tigers **193**.18
    in the UK **193**.31-2, 35, 36
    whales and dolphins **193**.29
    see also conservation; extinction; wildlife
endocrine disrupting chemicals **193**.16-17
endogenous (unipolar) depression **190**.10, 22-3
endometriosis **178**.4
energy
    and the countryside **97**.24-5
    and exercise **141**.39
    household costs and poverty **160**.22-3
    and meat-eating **140**.21
    output of the energy industry **97**.3

Volume numbers appear first (in bold) followed by page numbers; a change in volume number is preceded by a semi-**colon.**

Vol. 88 Food and Nutrition
Vol. 97 Energy Matters
Vol. 99 Exploited Children
Vol. 100 Stress and Anxiety
Vol. 119 Transport Trends
Vol. 129 Gambling Trends
Vol. 134 Customers and Consumerism
Vol. 138 A Genetically Modified Future?
Vol. 139 The Education Problem
Vol. 140 Vegetarian and Vegan Diets
Vol. 141 Mental Health
Vol. 142 Media Issues
Vol. 144 The Cloning Debate
Vol. 146 Sustainability and Environment
Vol. 147 The Terrorism Problem
Vol. 148 Religious Beliefs
Vol. 149 A Classless Society?
Vol. 150 Migration and Population
Vol. 151 Climate Change
Vol. 152 Euthanasia and the Right to Die
Vol. 153 Sexual Orientation and Society
Vol. 154 The Gender Gap
Vol. 155 Domestic Abuse

Vol. 156 Travel and Tourism
Vol. 157 The Problem of Globalisation
Vol. 158 The Internet Revolution
Vol. 159 An Ageing Population
Vol. 160 Poverty and Exclusion
Vol. 161 Waste Issues
Vol. 162 Staying Fit
Vol. 163 Drugs in the UK
Vol. 164 The AIDS Crisis
Vol. 165 Bullying Issues
Vol. 166 Marriage and Cohabitation
Vol. 167 Our Human Rights
Vol. 168 Privacy and Surveillance
Vol. 169 The Animal Rights Debate
Vol. 170 Body Image and Self-Esteem
Vol. 171 Abortion – Rights and Ethics
Vol. 172 Racial and Ethnic Discrimination
Vol. 173 Sexual Health
Vol. 174 Selling Sex
Vol. 175 Citizenship and Participation
Vol. 176 Health Issues for Young People
Vol. 177 Crime in the UK
Vol. 178 Reproductive Ethics

Vol. 179 Tackling Child Abuse
Vol. 180 Money and Finances
Vol. 181 The Housing Issue
Vol. 182 Teenage Conceptions
Vol. 183 Work and Employment
Vol. 184 Understanding Eating Disorders
Vol. 185 Student Matters
Vol. 186 Cannabis Use
Vol. 187 Health and the State
Vol. 188 Tobacco and Health
Vol. 189 The Homeless Population
Vol. 190 Coping with Depression
Vol. 191 The Changing Family
Vol. 192 Bereavement and Grief
Vol. 193 Endangered Species
Vol. 194 Responsible Drinking
Vol. 195 Alternative Medicine
Vol. 196 Censorship Issues
Vol. 197 Living with Disability
Vol. 198 Sport and Society
Vol. 199 Self-Harming and Suicide

production and supply **97**.3-4
public attitudes to energy and environment **97**.34-6
saving through recycling **161**.22
from waste **161**.20, 38, 39
energy consumption **97**.6
construction industry **146**.11
increasing **146**.39
energy dependence of UK **146**.5-6
energy efficiency **97**.27-33; **151**.29
and global warming **97**.29
in the home **97**.2, 27-30, 31, 32-3; **151**.39; **181**.39
and renewable energy sources **97**.11
and shopping **97**.31-2
and sustainable housing **181**.39
and transport **97**.24, 25, 31
see also renewable energy
England
biodiversity loss **193**.31-2
Biodiversity Strategy **146**.33
flag **131**.4
homelessness statistics **189**.3
NHS provision **187**.29, 30
rough sleepers **189**.16
teenage pregnancy **182**.2, 7, 10
English language, diversification **157**.16
English people
awareness of constitutional change **131**.5
British identity **131**.6
entertainment and the Internet **158**.3, 7, 21-2
entrepreneurship aspirations **183**.7
environment
and agriculture **146**.25
and air travel **156**.21, 26
effects of genetic modification **138**.12-14, 24
effect of globalisation **157**.10
information requests **142**.19
and meat production **140**.13, 16-7
effect of migration **150**.26-7
effect of non-agricultural market access (NAMA) **157**.14
protection of **88**.32, 34, 35
public attitudes to **97**.34
sustainable housing **181**.39
impact of tourism **156**.20, 21, 22, 25
air travel **156**.21, 26
reducing **156**.24
and transnational companies **157**.10-11
and urban growth **146**.17
and World Trade Organization **157**.22-3
see also sustainable development; wildlife
environmental globalisation **157**.2
environmental governance, international **193**.12
environmental migration **146**.16-17
environmental motoring, Ford **134**.30
environmental sustainability *see* sustainability
environmental taxes **157**.12-13
environmental tobacco smoke *see* passive smoking
environmentally cleaner vehicles **119**.20-23
ephebiphobia (fear of young people) **177**.22
epilepsy and exercise **198**.23
equal pay *see* gender pay gap
Equality Act **153**.35; **183**.13

equality at work **183**.12, 26-7
established church **148**.21-2
estimates and consumer rights **134**.18
ethical consumerism **134**.30-38
ethical food **134**.32, 34-7
ethical trade **134**.36; **157**.18
see also fair trade
ethical travel **134**.30
ethics
and animal experiments **169**.15-16
of genetic modification **138**.23
of human cloning **144**.2-3, 5-6, 7-8
ethnic groups interaction **147**.19
ethnic minorities
British identity **115**.38
and community feelings **131**.2
and country of birth **131**.8
and education **115**.18; **139**.8-9
interest in the news **142**.32-3
and mental illness **141**.23
mixed race population in the UK **115**.24-5
and national identity **131**.1, 8
and racial discrimination perception **131**.2-3
social mobility **149**.21-2
and the UK census **115**.3
as victims of crime **115**.10
see also Asian people; black people; employment and racism; racism
ethnic origin
and age of population, UK **150**.39
census data **150**.36
and education **139**.8-9
gender and educational achievement **154**.23
gender and pupil behaviour **154**.24
as grounds for discrimination **115**.7
and poverty **160**.2
rough sleepers **189**.17
women in the workforce **154**.29
Europe
human rights treaties **168**.3
IVF availability **178**.8
online gambling **129**.20
slavery **167**.20
European Commission on Human Rights **167**.4; **168**.3
European Convention on Human Rights **167**.4
and privacy **168**.3
and sexuality **153**.30-31
European Convention on Human Rights and Biomedicine **144**.11
European countries, press freedom **196**.2
European Court of Human Rights **153**.31
and DNA records **168**.12
and gay adoption **153**.31
and parental rights **153**.34
and privacy **168**.3
European Union
accession countries, migration from **150**.6-7
and biotechnology **138**.28-9
carbon credits **151**.35, 37
Charter of Fundamental Rights Related to Technological Innovation **142**.1

child abuse laws **179**.29
citizenship **131**.38
complementary medicine research **195**.16
and corporal punishment legislation **179**.31
elections **131**.15
entry-exit system **168**.9
GM ban, effect on developing countries **138**.29-30
human rights treaties **168**.3
and ID cards **131**.13
students from EU countries **139**.30, 32
surveillance in **168**.9
trafficking laws **179**.29
views of young people **131**.39
and wildlife trade **146**.34
workplace gender gap **154**.17-18, 33
euthanasia **152**.1-39
    active **152**.5
    arguments against **152**.3-4, 5, 17-18
    arguments for **152**.3-4, 6, 10
    and treatment of babies **152**.4, 32, 33, 34
    definitions **152**.1, 2, 5, 19
    diminishing respect for life **152**.3-4
    involuntary **152**.1
    law on **152**.1, 16-18, 29-30
    medical profession's attitudes **152**.7, 8, 24-6, 27-8
    non-voluntary **152**.1, 3
    in other countries **152**.4, 18, 19, 31, 33
    and religious faith **152**.7, 12, 15
        Church of England **152**.34
        Roman Catholic Church **152**.3-4
    statistics **152**.17, 23, 24, 25
    see also advance directives; assisted suicide; physician
        assisted suicide (PAS)
eviction of tenants **181**.16
evidence obtained under torture **167**.27
evolution, public opinions on **148**.37
ex-service personnel and homelessness **189**.6
exams **139**.4
    results
        A-levels **139**.18
        academies **139**.14, 15
        AS-levels **139**.18

exceeding expectation **139**.22
    GCSEs **139**.2
gender differences **154**.22, 23
    and single-sex schooling **139**.12; **154**.27
standards **139**.19-20
and stress **100**.3-7; **176**.5, 38-9
    causes of **100**.5
    dealing with **100**.5, 6
    getting help and advice with **100**.3
    see also A-levels; AS-levels; GCSEs
exchange rate, effect on tourism **156**.1, 7-8
exclusion clauses and consumer rights **134**.19-20
exclusions from school
    black pupils **115**.19-20; **139**.9
    and ethnicity **139**.8, 9
    gender differences **154**.24
exercise **88**.1, 2-3, 11, 12, 18; **162**.6; 29-34; **176**.6-7
    and the ageing process **159**.33; **162**.12
    barriers to **162**.24, 29
    and body image **176**.7
    children **119**.31; **162**.6, 26, 28, 29; **176**.3
        effect on weight **162**.28, 29
        lack of exercise **162**.13, 15, 25
    compulsive **162**.39; **184**.7
    and depression **162**.37, 38; **190**.3, 7, 38
    and eating disorders **184**.32
    government strategy **162**.18
    and health **162**.11-12, 29-31
    and health problems **198**.23
    influence of lads' magazines **170**.28
    lack of see inactivity
    and life expectancy **159**.33
    and mental health **141**.34, 39; **162**.37, 38; **190**.3, 38
    motivation for **162**.30-31
    and obesity **162**.28, 29, 36
    older people **159**.39
    and pregnancy **182**.15
    recommended amounts **162**.30
    statistics **162**.6
    and stress
        benefits of **100**.19, 27, 30, 34, 36, 37
    and weight loss **162**.20

Volume numbers appear first (in bold) followed by page numbers; a change in volume number is preceded by a semi-**colon.**

Vol. 88 Food and Nutrition
Vol. 97 Energy Matters
Vol. 99 Exploited Children
Vol. 100 Stress and Anxiety
Vol. 119 Transport Trends
Vol. 129 Gambling Trends
Vol. 134 Customers and Consumerism
Vol. 138 A Genetically Modified Future?
Vol. 139 The Education Problem
Vol. 140 Vegetarian and Vegan Diets
Vol. 141 Mental Health
Vol. 142 Media Issues
Vol. 144 The Cloning Debate
Vol. 146 Sustainability and Environment
Vol. 147 The Terrorism Problem
Vol. 148 Religious Beliefs
Vol. 149 A Classless Society?
Vol. 150 Migration and Population
Vol. 151 Climate Change
Vol. 152 Euthanasia and the Right to Die
Vol. 153 Sexual Orientation and Society
Vol. 154 The Gender Gap
Vol. 155 Domestic Abuse

Vol. 156 Travel and Tourism
Vol. 157 The Problem of Globalisation
Vol. 158 The Internet Revolution
Vol. 159 An Ageing Population
Vol. 160 Poverty and Exclusion
Vol. 161 Waste Issues
Vol. 162 Staying Fit
Vol. 163 Drugs in the UK
Vol. 164 The AIDS Crisis
Vol. 165 Bullying Issues
Vol. 166 Marriage and Cohabitation
Vol. 167 Our Human Rights
Vol. 168 Privacy and Surveillance
Vol. 169 The Animal Rights Debate
Vol. 170 Body Image and Self-Esteem
Vol. 171 Abortion – Rights and Ethics
Vol. 172 Racial and Ethnic Discrimination
Vol. 173 Sexual Health
Vol. 174 Selling Sex
Vol. 175 Citizenship and Participation
Vol. 176 Health Issues for Young People
Vol. 177 Crime in the UK
Vol. 178 Reproductive Ethics

Vol. 179 Tackling Child Abuse
Vol. 180 Money and Finances
Vol. 181 The Housing Issue
Vol. 182 Teenage Conceptions
Vol. 183 Work and Employment
Vol. 184 Understanding Eating Disorders
Vol. 185 Student Matters
Vol. 186 Cannabis Use
Vol. 187 Health and the State
Vol. 188 Tobacco and Health
Vol. 189 The Homeless Population
Vol. 190 Coping with Depression
Vol. 191 The Changing Family
Vol. 192 Bereavement and Grief
Vol. 193 Endangered Species
Vol. 194 Responsible Drinking
Vol. 195 Alternative Medicine
Vol. 196 Censorship Issues
Vol. 197 Living with Disability
Vol. 198 Sport and Society
Vol. 199 Self-Harming and Suicide

when not to exercise 162.31-2
    in the workplace 162.23, 24
    and young people 176.6-7
exhaust gases *see* emissions, transport
exotic species
    in the wild, Britain 193.39
    trade in 193.20-21
exploitation of workers
    migrant workers 150.14, 15, 19, 20, 22
extended schools 149.30, 37-8
extended warranties 134.19
external costs of motoring 119.14
extra-curricular activities and social mobility 149.30, 37-8
extremism
    monitoring extremist networks 147.13-14
    tackling 147.33-4; 148.30-31
extremist parties 131.23-4
    impact on democracy 131.24
eyes
    stem cell therapy 144.22
    test for Alzheimer's disease 141.19

F

Facebook
    censorship of sexual content 196.37
    and privacy 168.35
facial stem cell therapy 144.21-2
factory farming and animal cloning 144.35
FADS2 gene and ADHD 141.19
fair trade 134.34-7; 157.18, 27, 31-4
    coffee 157.32, 33
    cotton 157.28, 34
    ineffectiveness 157.34
Fairtrade Foundation 134.34-5, 36-7; 157.31
Fairtrade mark 134.35, 37
faith-based bullying 165.9
faith differences and relationships 115.39
faith hate crime 115.27
faith healing 195.5
faith schools 148.34, 35-6
    and sex education 173.34-5
fallopian tube damage and infertility 178.4
falls, older people 159.4, 6
false memory syndrome 179.26-9
families
    abuse of older people 159.17
    of cannabis users 186.23-5
    changing family patterns 166.15; 177.2; 191.1-4
    and debt problems 160.12
    digital technology usage 158.7-8
    of disabled young people 197.18-19
    of drug users 186.23-5
        support for 163.24
    equality issues 154.3
    family breakdown
        and children's wellbeing 191.9
        and paternal contact 191.11
        and youth homelessness 189.21, 26, 27
        see also divorce

family structure, effect on children's character 191.6
    and football 141.33
    and homelessness 189.29-32
    income, effect on educational attainment 149.25
    of lesbians and gay people, support 153.10
    low income, broadband access 158.18
    and the Mental Health Act 190.11
    and mobile phones 158.13
    and poverty 160.13-14
    reaction to mixed-faith relationships 115.39
    support during divorce 166.29, 30, 31
    support for pregnant teenagers 182.16
    see also lone parents; parents; stepfamilies
family group conferencing 177.31
family planning
    US overseas aid funding 171.13-14
    see also birth control; contraception
family planning clinics, use by teenagers 173.9; 182.1-2
Farm Scale Evaluation (FSE) trials 138.7, 13
farming *see* agriculture; organic farming
fashion industry
    employment conditions 157.27-9
    promoting unhealthy body size 184.24
fasting
    Christianity 148.10
    Islam 148.11
fat 162.8
    spot-reduction 162.33
fat intake 88.2, 5, 7, 8
    and food labelling 88.21-2, 22-3
    and red meat 140.12
fathers
    contact with children after family break-up 191.11
    parenting roles 191.30-33
    paternity leave 183.18, 22, 24; 191.34-5, 39
    post-natal depression 190.16-17
    teenage fathers 182.17
    work-family balance 183.22-3; 191.34-5
fatty acids
    and ADHD (attention-deficit hyperactivity disorder) 141.19
    in diet 141.30
fatwa 147.15
faulty goods, consumer rights 134.17
fear of crime 177.2, 6, 20-21
fear of terrorism 147.12
fear of young people 177.3, 22
feelings
    of animals 140.27-8
    after bereavement 192.1-2, 3, 9-10, 11, 13, 15, 20
fees, university 139.34; 185.11, 17, 29, 36
female condoms (femidom) 173.24
feminism
    and men 154.7-8
    as reason for not marrying 166.10
fertility
    effect of abortion 171.3
    effect of cannabis use 186.16
    and environmental stress 146.16-17
    problems 178.2-5
    UK 151.32

worldwide **150**.32-3, 34
fertility tourism **178**.18, 20
fertility treatment, gay people **153**.33-4
festivals
    Buddhism **148**.2
    Christianity **148**.2
    Hinduism **148**.3
    Islam **148**.3
    Judaism **148**.4
    Sikhism **148**.5
fetus
    age of viability **171**.23, 31, 33-4
    feeling pain **171**.31, 34
    religious views on foetus **171**.17-18
    testing for disability **171**.22
fibre intake **88**.2, 5, 6, 23
filesharing **158**.36
films
    classification **196**.13-16
        public opinion **196**.15-16
    influence on young people smoking **188**.25
    online viewing **158**.21-2
filtered cigarettes **188**.10
finance and football **198**.11-12
financial abuse and older people **159**.16
financial benefits *see* state benefits
financial companies, informing of a death **192**.32
financial crisis, global **180**.1-2
financial disruption to terrorism **147**.3, 28
financial education **180**.36-9
financial expectations, young people **180**.20-21
financial freedom, older people **159**.20
financial implications of partner's death **192**.33
financial incentives
    for health care **187**.37
    for marriage **166**.5; **191**.2
    for reducing waste **161**.38
    for weight loss **162**.22-3
financial planning for old age **159**.21-2; **180**.8
    see also pensions
financial products, expenditure on **134**.4
financial responsibility for children **166**.14-15, 34-5

financial support to adult children
    by parents **191**.27-8
fine particles, air pollution **146**.35
fines **177**.17, 24
fingerprinting
    on arrest **177**.36
    in schools **168**.30
fires caused by smoking **188**.22
first-time buyers
    parental support **181**.1
    pessimism about owning homes **181**.5
fisheries **146**.28
fishing and sustainability **146**.28-9; **193**.30
fitness
    effects on ageing **159**.33, 34; **162**.12
    equipment for older people **159**.39
    government strategy **162**.17-18
    inequalities **162**.35
    and mental health **141**.34, 39; **162**.37, 38
    motivation **162**.30-31
    myths **162**.33-4
fitness industry, lack of effect on obesity **162**.35
Five Freedoms (animal husbandry) **169**.12
fixed penalty notices **177**.8, 25
flags **131**.3-4
Fleet Street and newspaper publishing **142**.8-9
flexible working **183**.16-27
    effect of recession **183**.1
    fathers **183**.22; **191**.34, 39
    mothers **191**.36
    options **183**.17, 18
    statistics **183**.20
flooding and climate change **151**.10-11
fly-tipping **161**.16
foetal stem cells **144**.25
foetus *see* fetus
foil, aluminium, recycling **161**.27
folate, increased in GM tomatoes **138**.14
food
    and animal cloning **144**.36-9
    and energy efficiency **97**.32, 33
    ethical **134**.34-7

Volume numbers appear first (in bold) followed by page numbers; a change in volume number is preceded by a semi-**colon.**

Vol. 88 Food and Nutrition
Vol. 97 Energy Matters
Vol. 99 Exploited Children
Vol. 100 Stress and Anxiety
Vol. 119 Transport Trends
Vol. 129 Gambling Trends
Vol. 134 Customers and Consumerism
Vol. 138 A Genetically Modified Future?
Vol. 139 The Education Problem
Vol. 140 Vegetarian and Vegan Diets
Vol. 141 Mental Health
Vol. 142 Media Issues
Vol. 144 The Cloning Debate
Vol. 146 Sustainability and Environment
Vol. 147 The Terrorism Problem
Vol. 148 Religious Beliefs
Vol. 149 A Classless Society?
Vol. 150 Migration and Population
Vol. 151 Climate Change
Vol. 152 Euthanasia and the Right to Die
Vol. 153 Sexual Orientation and Society
Vol. 154 The Gender Gap
Vol. 155 Domestic Abuse

Vol. 156 Travel and Tourism
Vol. 157 The Problem of Globalisation
Vol. 158 The Internet Revolution
Vol. 159 An Ageing Population
Vol. 160 Poverty and Exclusion
Vol. 161 Waste Issues
Vol. 162 Staying Fit
Vol. 163 Drugs in the UK
Vol. 164 The AIDS Crisis
Vol. 165 Bullying Issues
Vol. 166 Marriage and Cohabitation
Vol. 167 Our Human Rights
Vol. 168 Privacy and Surveillance
Vol. 169 The Animal Rights Debate
Vol. 170 Body Image and Self-Esteem
Vol. 171 Abortion – Rights and Ethics
Vol. 172 Racial and Ethnic Discrimination
Vol. 173 Sexual Health
Vol. 174 Selling Sex
Vol. 175 Citizenship and Participation
Vol. 176 Health Issues for Young People
Vol. 177 Crime in the UK
Vol. 178 Reproductive Ethics

Vol. 179 Tackling Child Abuse
Vol. 180 Money and Finances
Vol. 181 The Housing Issue
Vol. 182 Teenage Conceptions
Vol. 183 Work and Employment
Vol. 184 Understanding Eating Disorders
Vol. 185 Student Matters
Vol. 186 Cannabis Use
Vol. 187 Health and the State
Vol. 188 Tobacco and Health
Vol. 189 The Homeless Population
Vol. 190 Coping with Depression
Vol. 191 The Changing Family
Vol. 192 Bereavement and Grief
Vol. 193 Endangered Species
Vol. 194 Responsible Drinking
Vol. 195 Alternative Medicine
Vol. 196 Censorship Issues
Vol. 197 Living with Disability
Vol. 198 Sport and Society
Vol. 199 Self-Harming and Suicide

food costs and animal welfare **169**.11-12
food security **146**.12-13
GM food *see* genetically modified (GM) crops
and mental health **141**.30-31, 34; **190**.3
organic **134**.31
and religion **148**.10-11
supplies and GM crops **138**.9, 10, 34-5
UK dependence on imports **146**.5
and young people **176**.8-9
food advertising and children **134**.10
food labelling **88**.9, 21-5
GM food **138**.11, 39
food and nutrition **88**.1-39
additives **88**.13-14, 34, 36, 38, 39
advertising and promotion **88**.10, 11, 19, 20, 35, 37
food poisoning **88**.14, 27-9
food safety **88**.26, 32, 34
healthy diet **88**.1-2, 5-7
junk food **88**.9-11
locally grown produce **88**.31, 33
nutrition information panels **88**.21, 22-3
teenagers **176**.8-9
food packaging
recycling tins **161**.27
food poisoning **88**.14, 27-9
food production
and intensive farming **140**.36-7
and meat consumption **140**.13, 16-17
and mental health **141**.30
food security **157**.5
food waste **161**.4, 10-11, 19
football
Asian players **198**.24
finance **198**.11-12
and girls' self-esteem **170**.39
and homophobia **198**.25, 26
and mental health **141**.32-3
and violence **198**.13
WAGs (wives and girlfriends) **198**.15-17
footwear for exercise **162**.32
forced labour **167**.20, 22
forced marriages **155**.16-18; **166**.17-20
children **167**.32
forced retirement **183**.14-15
foreign-born population
UK **150**.29, 30
worldwide **150**.33
Foreign and Commonwealth Office, counter-terrorism **147**.1
foreign investment **157**.37
foreign students and terrorism **147**.13-14
forests
and carbon sequestration **151**.26
effect of increased trade **157**.14
empty forest syndrome **193**.20
protection **193**.4
rainforest destruction **193**.1, 5
restoration **193**.15
and sustainability **146**.30-31
see also deforestation
forgotten working poor **160**.22-3
fossil fuels
alternatives to reliance on **97**.2, 21
as an energy source **97**.8, 21
and biomass **97**.18
sustainable **151**.28-30
see also oil
fostering, by gay people **153**.34
foundation stage education, gender gap **154**.23
fox hunting **169**.27-36
France
gay adoption **153**.31
online retail sales **134**.15
fraud
phishing **134**.27-8, 28-9
scams **134**.26-8
free choice *see* autonomy
free newspapers **142**.9
free-range eggs **140**.6, 29
consumer choice **140**.37-8
and health **140**.30
production **140**.29, 38-9
free speech **196**.1-12
and the Internet **158**.2
free trade **157**.12-14, 17-18
benefits **157**.25
and developing countries **157**.20, 25, 26-7
effect on employment **157**.13, 23
effect on poverty **157**.9, 13
freedom of expression **196**.37
and cartoons of Muhammed **142**.34
Freedom Food mark **140**.29, 34
fish **146**.29
Freedom of Information Act **142**.18-20; **168**.10-11
delays in meeting requests **142**.20
and regional newspapers **142**.17
freedom of information **196**.38
complaints **168**.4
freedom of the press, global study **196**.1-2
freedom from surveillance **196**.38
freezing
eggs **178**.23
embryos **178**.22
freight transport trends **119**.1
freshwater resources **193**.5
friends, bullied, how to help **165**.6
friendship
and football **141**.33
and mental health **141**.28-9
fruit and vegetable consumption **162**.6
fruit machines **129**.2
and under 16s **129**.11
fruitarian diet **140**.2
fuel cell vehicles **119**.22-3
fuel efficient cars **119**.20-23
fuel poverty **160**.22-3
pensioners **159**.3
fuel taxes **119**.14, 24
aircraft **119**.16
fuels, cleaner **119**.20-23
full-time parents, stress **191**.35
fundamentalism, Islam **147**.15
funding

academies **139**.14

BBC **142**.6

higher education **185**.17, 35-6

 see also tuition fees

HIV prevention programmes **164**.23, 39

human rights programmes **167**.5

NHS **187**.1, 3, 11-12, 30

 and homeopathy **195**.16, 17-22, 24-5

security services **147**.2

sport

 disability sports **198**.18, 20, 21

 funding cuts **198**.6-7

students **139**.34-5

funerals **192**.30-31, 34-7

 environmental **134**.31

fur trade **169**.5-8

furnishings, spending on **134**.4

furniture recycling **161**.24

further education **139**.2

benefits of **183**.33, 34

G

G7 and G8 countries **157**.5

G8 summit

 climate change accord **151**.16-17

Galapagos Islands, environmental change **193**.24-5

gambling **129**.1-39

 addiction *see* compulsive gambling

 addictiveness **129**.30

 benefits **129**.18

 controlled **129**.2, 28

 definition **129**.1, 28

 effects **129**.36

  physical **129**.29, 36

  psychological **129**.6, 29

  research **129**.16

 expenditure on **129**.4

  children **129**.32, 33

  mobile gambling **129**.26

  National Lottery **129**.9, 10

online gambling **129**.17, 19

forms of **129**.2

 licence conditions **129**.8, 23

history of **129**.1

and law

 Gambling Act **129**.5, 17, 23

 and gambling at work **129**.23

 online gambling **129**.17

licensing **129**.5, 8, 23

by mobiles **129**.18, 26

and neurobiology **129**.6

online gambling **129**.17-18, 19-25

participation in **129**.4

 National Lottery **129**.9, 10

 online gambling **129**.19

 young people **129**.11

problem gamblers *see* compulsive gambling

psychology of **129**.6, 29

signs of problems **129**.22-3, 24, 28, 29, 35-6, 38

social factors **129**.7, 29

statistics **129**.1-3, 4

underage **129**.1

 National Lottery **129**.11-13

 online gambling **129**.18, 25

 online poker **129**.25

 Scotland **129**.32-3

at work **129**.22-4

women **129**.21, 27, 34

young people **129**.1

 addiction **129**.25, 31, 32-3

 National Lottery **129**.11-13

 signs of gambling problems **129**.38

 views on gambling **129**.13

gamete intrafallopian transfer (GIFT) **178**.11

gamete market **178**.12

gaming

 addiction to **158**.39

 concerns about violence **158**.33

gamma-butyrolactone (GBL) **194**.9

gamma-hydroxybutyrate (GHB) **194**.9

Gang Activity Desistance Orders (GADOs) **177**.9

gangs **177**.9-10, 12-14; **189**.28

dealing with **177**.9-10, 14
definition **177**.10
signs of membership **177**.12-13
gap years **156**.15-19; **185**.31; **183**.20
garment companies, working conditions **157**.27-9
gastric surgery for weight loss **162**.3
GATS (General Agreement on Trade and Services) **157**.6
GATT (General Agreement on Trade and Tariffs) **157**.5-6
gay adoption **153**.31-2
gay couples
adoption and fostering **153**.34
fertility treatment **153**.33-4
having a child **153**.20-22; **178**.9-10
gay gene theory **153**.6
gay issues in children's literature **153**.19-20
gay men
and adoption **191**.22-5
in boardroom positions **153**.39
and HIV **96**.17, 20, 23; **164**.22
HIV prevention campaigns **164**.24
infection rate **164**.16, 17, 22
life expectancy **164**.9
and the media **142**.39
and sexually transmitted infections (STIs) **96**.3, 4, 10, 12
GCSEs **139**.4
academies **139**.14, 15
and ethnicity **139**.8
gender differences **154**.22
results **139**.2
GDP (Gross Domestic Product) **157**.6
as measure of living standards **157**.13
gender
and alcohol consumption, young people **194**.2
and alcohol-related deaths **194**.13
and Alzheimer's disease **159**.36
and attitudes to sex **173**.12-13
and car use **119**.29
and child pedestrian accidents **119**.5
and compulsive shopping **134**.14
definition **154**.1
development **154**.1
differences **154**.1, 9
and drug abuse **163**.29-30
and education *see* gender and education
and graduate unemployment **185**.32
and household financial roles **180**.18-19
and mental health problems **141**.1; **190**.18-19
and online shopping **134**.16
and parental roles **191**.30-32
and pay *see* gender pay gap
and schizophrenia **141**.4
and smoking **188**.1
and society **154**.1-14
and stress **100**.13, 19
and suicide **199**.24, 28, 32
and work **154**.29-35
see also gender pay gap; men; women
gender-based violence **154**.12
see also domestic abuse; rape
gender and education **139**.10-11; **154**.22-7
A-level performance **139**.18

and educational performance **139**.2; **154**.22, 23
higher education **139**.32; **185**.14
reasons for gender gap **154**.25
subject choices **139**.11; **154**.26
worldwide **154**.12
gender equality
changes since 1970s **154**.5
goals **154**.2-4, 6
Millennium Development Goals **160**.13
Olympic Games **198**.19
and Oxfam programmes **154**.12
gender inequality **154**.2-4
and HIV **164**.5-6
worldwide **154**.12-14
gender pay gap **154**.2-3, 6, 30, 35-9
graduates **139**.36
senior management **154**.38
gender power gap **154**.4, 6
gender-specific behaviour **154**.1, 9
gender stereotypes
and bullying **165**.12-13
in careers advice **154**.28
male **154**.7-8
gender and work **154**.29-35
careers advice **154**.28, 35
and pay *see* gender pay gap
see also women in the workforce
General Agreement on Trade and Services (GATS) **157**.6
General Agreement on Trade and Tariffs (GATT) **157**.5-6
general practitioners *see* GPs (general practitioners)
gene doping **198**.30
gene splicing *see* genetic modification
General Elections **131**.18
genes **138**.4, 12; **178**.3
and addiction **141**.9
and ageing **159**.2, 32
and Alzheimer's disease **159**.36
and attention-deficit hyperactivity disorder (ADHD) **141**.19
and depression **190**.2, 4, 12-13
bipolar disorder **190**.11, 12-13
teenage depression **190**.25
and obesity **162**.9-10
and sexuality **153**.6, 7
genetic barriers **144**.12
genetic biodiversity **146**.18
genetic engineering **144**.20
genetic modification
definition **138**.1, 2, 4
and the environment **138**.12-14, 24
ethical issues **138**.23
limitations **138**.37-8
product labeling **138**.11, 25, 39
public attitudes to **138**.3, 15-16
technologies **138**.35
Genetic Use Restriction Technologies (GURTs) **138**.18
genetically modified animals, experiments on **144**.34; **169**.16, 17
genetically modified (GM) crops **88**.14, 32, 33; **146**.26-7
and animal feed **138**.25
benefits of **138**.8-10

crop area **138**.2, 25, 29
cross-contamination **138**.6-7, 12-13
developing countries **138**.9, 10, 23, 29-30, 34-5
drug crops (pharming) **138**.4, 9-10, 20-22
and food production **140**.37
future for **138**.13; **146**.26-7
land register proposal **138**.36
non-food crops **138**.10, 14
potato research trials **138**.27, 28
rice **138**.20, 31-4
risks **138**.8-10, 24
safety **138**.6
tobacco plants **138**.21-2
UK **138**.2-3, 5, 39
genetically modified organisms (GMOs)
benefits **138**.12
concerns about **138**.12-13, 24
definition **138**.4, 12
hens **138**.20-21
see also genetically modified crops
genital herpes **173**.18, 21
genital warts **173**.18, 20-21
Genito-Urinary Medicine (GUM) clinics **96**.1, 10
health advisers and safer sex **96**.1, 10
and HIV testing **96**.16
pressure on services **96**.3, 4, 8-9, 11
tests and treatment offered at **96**.10
genomics **138**.2-3, 37-9
geothermal energy **97**.6-7, 9, 11-12
germ line therapy **144**.20
germ line transmission **144**.26
Germany
extremist parties **131**.23
online retail sales **134**.15
germs **88**.27, 28-9
gestational surrogacy **178**.7, 13
ghettos **115**.28, 31
GIFT (gamete intrafallopian transfer) **178**.11
gifted and talented scheme, and black pupils **139**.9
girls' schools **154**.27
girls and young women
aspiring to be WAGS **198**.15-17

attitudes to sex **173**.12-13
and beauty salons **170**.25-6
and body image **170**.21-2, 24; **184**.17-18, 27
careers information **154**.28, 35
and child labour **99**.2, 3
child soldiers **99**.29, 31, 36
and cosmetic surgery **170**.32-3
and cricket **198**.4
dieting **184**.22
discrimination against **154**.13-14
drug abuse **163**.29-30
and education **154**.22-6
examination results **154**.22, 23
foundation stage **154**.23
single-sex education **154**.27
subject choices **154**.22, 26
effects of mother's dieting **184**.21-2
and mental health problems **141**.1
sexual exploitation of **99**.16, 20, 21-2
sexualisation of **154**.10
sport and self-esteem **170**.39
street children **99**.18-19
violence against **154**.13-14; **155**.26
glass **161**.5, 22
recycling **161**.24, 27
glass ceiling **154**.38
for gay people **153**.39
glass cliff **154**.34
global citizenship **131**.37
global financial crisis **180**.1-2
Global Gag Rule **171**.13-14
global gender inequality **154**.12-14
global inequality **160**.26, 29
global interdependence **146**.4-6
global positioning system (GPS)
and road charging **119**.36
and surveillance
global poverty **160**.25-39
global trade, attitudes to **157**.39
global warming **151**.1
and air travel **156**.26
and biodiversity **146**.19

Volume numbers appear first (in bold) followed by page numbers; a change in volume number is preceded by a semi-**colon.**

Vol. 88 Food and Nutrition
Vol. 97 Energy Matters
Vol. 99 Exploited Children
Vol. 100 Stress and Anxiety
Vol. 119 Transport Trends
Vol. 129 Gambling Trends
Vol. 134 Customers and Consumerism
Vol. 138 A Genetically Modified Future?
Vol. 139 The Education Problem
Vol. 140 Vegetarian and Vegan Diets
Vol. 141 Mental Health
Vol. 142 Media Issues
Vol. 144 The Cloning Debate
Vol. 146 Sustainability and Environment
Vol. 147 The Terrorism Problem
Vol. 148 Religious Beliefs
Vol. 149 A Classless Society?
Vol. 150 Migration and Population
Vol. 151 Climate Change
Vol. 152 Euthanasia and the Right to Die
Vol. 153 Sexual Orientation and Society
Vol. 154 The Gender Gap
Vol. 155 Domestic Abuse

Vol. 156 Travel and Tourism
Vol. 157 The Problem of Globalisation
Vol. 158 The Internet Revolution
Vol. 159 An Ageing Population
Vol. 160 Poverty and Exclusion
Vol. 161 Waste Issues
Vol. 162 Staying Fit
Vol. 163 Drugs in the UK
Vol. 164 The AIDS Crisis
Vol. 165 Bullying Issues
Vol. 166 Marriage and Cohabitation
Vol. 167 Our Human Rights
Vol. 168 Privacy and Surveillance
Vol. 169 The Animal Rights Debate
Vol. 170 Body Image and Self-Esteem
Vol. 171 Abortion – Rights and Ethics
Vol. 172 Racial and Ethnic Discrimination
Vol. 173 Sexual Health
Vol. 174 Selling Sex
Vol. 175 Citizenship and Participation
Vol. 176 Health Issues for Young People
Vol. 177 Crime in the UK
Vol. 178 Reproductive Ethics

Vol. 179 Tackling Child Abuse
Vol. 180 Money and Finances
Vol. 181 The Housing Issue
Vol. 182 Teenage Conceptions
Vol. 183 Work and Employment
Vol. 184 Understanding Eating Disorders
Vol. 185 Student Matters
Vol. 186 Cannabis Use
Vol. 187 Health and the State
Vol. 188 Tobacco and Health
Vol. 189 The Homeless Population
Vol. 190 Coping with Depression
Vol. 191 The Changing Family
Vol. 192 Bereavement and Grief
Vol. 193 Endangered Species
Vol. 194 Responsible Drinking
Vol. 195 Alternative Medicine
Vol. 196 Censorship Issues
Vol. 197 Living with Disability
Vol. 198 Sport and Society
Vol. 199 Self-Harming and Suicide

causes of **151**.3-4, 5-6
computer models **151**.5
and consumer behaviour **134**.31
costs **151**.8
denial of **151**.14-15
effects of **151**.1, 7, 8
and energy efficiency **97**.29
evidence for **151**.1, 3
and renewable energy **97**.8
globalisation **157**.1-15
benefits **157**.1, 25, 26-7
and child labour **99**.14
concerns about **157**.3, 9-11, 25, 37-8
definition **157**.1, 2, 3, 6, 12
and developing countries **157**.25
and economic growth **157**.1
effects of **157**.1, 3-4, 9-11, 12, 37-8
and the environment **157**.10
facts **157**.2
and inequality **157**.3-4, 9
monoculture fears **157**.11
and multinationals **157**.30-31
and trade **157**.17-39
types **157**.2
glucose **88**.15
GM crops *see* genetically modified (GM) crops
GNP (Gross National Product) **157**.6
GNVQs (General National Vocational Qualifications) **139**.4
Golden Rule **148**.8-9, 15-16
gonorrhoea **173**.18, 21
'good' deaths **192**.8, 24
Google
Google Earth **168**.26-7
government censorship requests **196**.29
withdrawal from China **196**.27, 28, 29, 30
governance benefits of globalisation **157**.1
Government
and broadcasters **196**.18-19
the Budget **180**.24
control of the media **142**.2
finance, and smoking **188**.22, 23
funding for disabled children **197**.36
funding for higher education **180**.28, 33
media influence **142**.2
Parliament **131**.15
spending on aid **157**.10
surveillance **168**.4-5, 7-8, 13-14, 27, 35
Government policies
on alcohol **194**.33
on drugs **163**.22-4; **186**.4, 35-6
on genetically modified crops **138**.5
on health **162**.4-5, 9-10, 17-18, 22-3
on higher education **185**.25
on homelessness **189**.8, 34
on homeopathy **195**.24-5, 26-7
on housing **181**.23
missing affordable housing target **181**.6
houses of multiple occupation **181**.19-20
on integrated healthcare **195**.23
on plastic bags **161**.14
to reduce educational attainment gap **149**.30, 37-8

on sexually transmitted infections **173**.21
on smacking **179**.33
on smoking **188**.33-5
waste strategy **161**.20
Government targets
homelessness **189**.8
road safety **119**.4
governments
control of Internet **196**.32-5
Internet censorship requests **196**.29
role in globalisation **157**.4
and the World Trade Organization **157**.21
GPs (general practitioners)
and abortions **171**.25-6
asking about patient's alcohol consumption **194**.33, 37-8
diagnosing depression **190**.31
and eating disorders **184**.36
patient survey **187**.16-17
registering at university **176**.5
relationship with patients **187**.31
seeking help for stress from **100**.2, 33, 34
surgery waiting times **187**.16
see also doctors
GPS *see* global positioning system
graduates
basic skills concerns **139**.17
debt **139**.35
destinations **185**.31-2
earnings **139**.35, 36, 37; **183**.34; **185**.21, 32-4
employment **139**.33; **185**.31-2, 36-7
effect of recession **183**.1-2, 35-6
and social class **149**.2
incentives for teacher training **139**.12
options after graduating **185**.30-31
starting salaries **139**.35, 36; **183**.36
unemployment **180**.35
grandparents **191**.14-17
and childcare **191**.15, 16-17
grants, student **139**.34; **180**.28, 33; **185**.2
green belt land **181**.21, 36
green cars *see* fuel efficient cars
green consumerism **146**.38-9
green infrastructure **181**.36
green space and mental health **141**.35
green waste **161**.28-9, 30
greenfield development **181**.22, 36
greenhouse effect **151**.1, 3
greenhouse gases **151**.1, 7
emission reduction targets **146**.8-9
emissions, China **146**.5
emissions from tourism **156**.25
sequestration **151**.26
see also carbon dioxide emissions
grey squirrels **193**.38
grief **192**.1-2, 3-4
before death **192**.6
public **192**.7-8
and young people **192**.9-23
grooming, online **179**.16
Gross Domestic Product (GDP) **157**.6
Gross National Product (GNP) **157**.6

growth hormones and sports drug abuse **198**.30

guarantees, consumer rights **134**.18-19

guilt, children's feelings after bereavement **192**.13

gun crime **177**.15-16, 29-30

    young people's concerns **177**.15-16

guns and the law **177**.7

GURTs (Genetic Use Restriction Technologies) **138**.18

Gypsy/Roma children and education **115**.18

H

habitat loss **193**.1

    see also deforestation

haematopoietic cell transplantation (HTD) **144**.21

haemophiliacs and HIV **164**.25

hair, stem cell therapy **144**.22

hallucinogens (psychedelics) **163**.2, 6

hangovers **194**.7

    and exercise **162**.32

happiness

    of children, effect of paretnal relationship **166**.32

    in marriage **166**.7-8

    teaching in schools **170**.14-15

happy slapping **165**.31

haram foods, Islam **148**.11

harassment

    racial **115**.8

    on grounds of sexual orientation **153**.38

hard segregation **115**.28

hardening hypothesis (stopping smoking) **188**.17

hashish (cannabis resins) **186**.2, 7, 9

hazardous waste **161**.6, 32

hazardous work

    and child labour **99**.1, 2, 3

    domestic labour **99**.7

head injuries and risk of Alzheimer's disease **159**.36

headteachers, gender gap **154**.25

health **176**.1-39

    and alcohol

        benefits **194**.18

        risks **194**.6, 7, 15, 17, 18, 19, 22-3

    and body image **170**.23, 38

    and cannabis **163**.6, 9, 35; **186**.15-17, 28-9

    census information **150**.36

    and cloning **144**.2, 6, 39

    and compulsive exercise **162**.39

    and cycling **119**.39

    and drugs

        amphetamines **163**.4-5

        cocaine **163**.4

        ecstasy **163**.5, 10

        LSD **163**.6

        opiates **163**.5

        solvents **163**.6

    exercising with health problems **198**.23

    gender gap **154**.6

    and GM crops **138**.9-10

        see also pharming

    government strategies **162**.4-5, 9-10, 17-18, 22-3

    holidays **156**.4-5

    and homelessness **189**.12-13

    and marital status **166**.15

    and meat consumption **140**.12, 13, 21

    and migrants **150**.21-3

    and obesity **162**.1-2, 5, 6, 7, 19, 25

    older people **159**.4, 6, 8, 34

    and poverty **160**.2

    in pregnancy **182**.15

        employment rights **191**.37

    and smoking **188**.5-12, 15, 18, 19, 22

        benefits of giving up **188**.6, 9

        passive smoking **188**.5, 10-11, 12

        in pregnancy **188**.11, 31

    and social class **149**.13-14

    students **176**.5-6

    teenage parents and their children **182**.27

    tobacco pickers **188**.39

    and traffic increase **119**.1

    and traffic pollution **119**.13-14, 31

    UK health profile **187**.4, 11

    and vegetarian diets **140**.1, 2-3, 5, 11

    and walking to school **119**.27, 31

    young carers **141**.24

Volume numbers appear first (in bold) followed by page numbers; a change in volume number is preceded by a semi-**colon.**

Vol. 88 Food and Nutrition
Vol. 97 Energy Matters
Vol. 99 Exploited Children
Vol. 100 Stress and Anxiety
Vol. 119 Transport Trends
Vol. 129 Gambling Trends
Vol. 134 Customers and Consumerism
Vol. 138 A Genetically Modified Future?
Vol. 139 The Education Problem
Vol. 140 Vegetarian and Vegan Diets
Vol. 141 Mental Health
Vol. 142 Media Issues
Vol. 144 The Cloning Debate
Vol. 146 Sustainability and Environment
Vol. 147 The Terrorism Problem
Vol. 148 Religious Beliefs
Vol. 149 A Classless Society?
Vol. 150 Migration and Population
Vol. 151 Climate Change
Vol. 152 Euthanasia and the Right to Die
Vol. 153 Sexual Orientation and Society
Vol. 154 The Gender Gap
Vol. 155 Domestic Abuse

Vol. 156 Travel and Tourism
Vol. 157 The Problem of Globalisation
Vol. 158 The Internet Revolution
Vol. 159 An Ageing Population
Vol. 160 Poverty and Exclusion
Vol. 161 Waste Issues
Vol. 162 Staying Fit
Vol. 163 Drugs in the UK
Vol. 164 The AIDS Crisis
Vol. 165 Bullying Issues
Vol. 166 Marriage and Cohabitation
Vol. 167 Our Human Rights
Vol. 168 Privacy and Surveillance
Vol. 169 The Animal Rights Debate
Vol. 170 Body Image and Self-Esteem
Vol. 171 Abortion – Rights and Ethics
Vol. 172 Racial and Ethnic Discrimination
Vol. 173 Sexual Health
Vol. 174 Selling Sex
Vol. 175 Citizenship and Participation
Vol. 176 Health Issues for Young People
Vol. 177 Crime in the UK
Vol. 178 Reproductive Ethics

Vol. 179 Tackling Child Abuse
Vol. 180 Money and Finances
Vol. 181 The Housing Issue
Vol. 182 Teenage Conceptions
Vol. 183 Work and Employment
Vol. 184 Understanding Eating Disorders
Vol. 185 Student Matters
Vol. 186 Cannabis Use
Vol. 187 Health and the State
Vol. 188 Tobacco and Health
Vol. 189 The Homeless Population
Vol. 190 Coping with Depression
Vol. 191 The Changing Family
Vol. 192 Bereavement and Grief
Vol. 193 Endangered Species
Vol. 194 Responsible Drinking
Vol. 195 Alternative Medicine
Vol. 196 Censorship Issues
Vol. 197 Living with Disability
Vol. 198 Sport and Society
Vol. 199 Self-Harming and Suicide

health beliefs **150**.21-2
health care
    discrimination, disabled people **197**.30, 38-9
    eating disorders treatment **184**.12, 33-9
    effect of legalising euthanasia **152**.4
    health checks as legal right **187**.32-3
    NHS **187**.1-23
        future proposals **187**.32-9
        problems **187**.25-31
    older people **159**.6
    UK dependence on workers from overseas **146**.6
health cure scams **134**.27
health education on smoking **176**.13
health and safety issues, WTO **157**.23
health warnings on cigarette packs **188**.29
health and wellness holidays **156**.4-5
healthy eating **88**.1-2, 5-7; **184**.32
    children **162**.25-6; **176**.3
    government strategies **162**.10, 17-18
    and meat consumption **140**.12, 14, 21
    obsession with healthy eating **184**.9
    and social class **162**.13-14
    and stress relief **100**.30, 31, 34, 35, 38-9
    tyranny **162**.16
    and vegetarian diets **140**.1, 3-4, , 6, 7, 10, 11
    young people **176**.3, 8-9
hearing, stem cell therapy **144**.22
heart
    effects of alcohol **194**.18
    effects of smoking **188**.7
heart attacks and cycling **119**.39
heart disease
    and obesity **162**.7
    protective effect of alcohol **194**.18
    and smoking **188**.7
    stem cell therapy **144**.22, 23, 28
    and stress **100**.19
heatstroke and ecstasy **163**.10
heavy metals, air pollution **146**.36
hens
    genetically modified **138**.20-21
    welfare **140**.38-9
    see also free-range eggs
hepatitis **173**.18
herbal cannabis (marijuana/grass) **186**.2, 9
    see also skunk
herbal medicine **195**.3-4, 9, 10-13
    benefits **195**.11
    buying over the Internet **195**.8, 39
    calls for regulation **195**.33, 34-5
    definitions **195**.11
    efficacy **195**.33
    history of **195**.10
    how it works **195**.11
    and the NHS **195**.11
    perceptions of risk **195**.34
    public attitudes **195**.34-5
    registration scheme **195**.4, 35, 38
    reporting adverse reactions **195**.38-9
    safety **195**.2, 12-13, 37-9
    usage **195**.34

herbicide tolerance **138**.4
heredity
    and Alzheimer's disease **159**.36
    and mental illness **141**.24
heroin **163**.5
    market trends **163**.25
herpes see genital herpes
heterosexism **165**.13-14
heterosexual HIV infection rate **164**.16, 17
hidden disabilities **197**.8-9
hidden homelessness **189**.4, 23
high blood pressure (hypertension) **88**.2, 9, 16
higher education **139**.2, 29-39
    alternatives options **185**.16-17
    and business **185**.34-6
    degree results **139**.33
    and earning power **185**.1, 21-2; **183**.34
    funding **139**.34; **180**.28, 33; **185**.17, 35-6
    and gender **185**.14
    Government policy **185**.25
    reform **185**.20-21
    and social class **149**.1-2
    statistics **139**.32
    value of **185**.1, 15-17
Highers (exams) **139**.4
Hinduism **148**.2-3
    and faith schools **148**.35-6
    festivals **148**.3
    food rules **148**.3, 11
    funerals **148**.3; **192**.35
hire purchase **134**.22; **180**.27
HIV (Human Immunodeficiency Virus) **164**.1-39
    and anti-gay prejudice **153**.2
    and child labour **99**.3
    and child soldiers **99**.31
    disability classification **197**.1
    education **164**.18, 23-4
    and migrant population **150**.22-3
    Millennium Development Goals **160**.32
    older people as carers **159**.5
    and parents of lesbians and gay people **153**.9
    and poverty **164**.10, 27
    prevention **164**.3, 23-39
        campaigns **164**.23-5
        and condoms **164**.3
        funding **164**.16, 39
        targets **164**.28
        worldwide access to prevention services **164**.39
    and the sexual exploitation of children **99**.16, 24
    signs and symptoms **164**.1-2
    testing for **164**.2, 20-21
    transmission **164**.1, 11
        criminal **164**.12-13
        mother-to-child **164**.3, 25, 27, 29-30, 31, 38
        through blood products **164**.1, 19-20, 25
    treatments **164**.2-3
        antiretroviral therapy (ART) **164**.2-3, 8-9, 29, 30-32
        combination therapy **164**.2-3, 8-9, 30-31
        drugs from GM (pharmed) crops **138**.21, 22
        side effects **164**.3, 31
        vaccines **164**.34-6

worldwide access **164**.38-9

UK statistics **164**.16, 17, 22; **173**.3, 21

and women **164**.5-6

   pregnant **164**.3, 25, 27, 29-30, 31

worldwide statistics **164**.4, 38-9

and young people **164**.18; **176**.4, 28

see also AIDS

HMOs (houses of multiple occupation) **181**.19-20

holidays

and climate change concerns **156**.28-30

destinations **156**.3

as economic indicator **180**.5

ethical **134**.30

expenditure on **134**.3

as status symbols **156**.5

see also responsible tourism; tourism

home abortions **171**.35-6

home building **181**.2

affordable homes **181**.6, 29

green belt land **181**.21

greenfield sites **181**.22, 26

self-build **181**.30-31

home care services **159**.4

   costs **159**.26

home expenditure, ethical **134**.32

home furnishings, spending on **134**.4

home information packs, political party policies **181**.23

home insulation **151**.38, 39

home learning **139**.27-8

Home Office and counter-terrorism **147**.2

home ownership

low-cost options **181**.25

pessimism about prospects **181**.5

and social class **149**.20

   attitudes to moving home **149**.26

and social housing tenants **181**.33-5

young people **181**.26

home schooling **139**.27

homelessness **189**.1-39

asylum seekers **189**.14-15

causes **189**.5, 6, 24, 26, 27

and children **189**.29-32

definitions **189**.1, 3

and drug use **189**.10-11, 13, 35-6

effects **189**.5

and employment **189**.33

and health **189**.12-13

government policies **189**.8, 34

help for homeless people **189**.34-9

hidden homeless **189**.4, 23

legislation **189**.1-2, 34

and local authorities **189**.1-2, 34

and mental health **189**.9-11

and older people **159**.4

priority needs groups **189**.2, 3

rough sleeping **189**.4, 16-17

   Government targets **189**.8

   and mental health **189**.11

   young people **189**.23

statistics **189**.3-4, 16-17, 21, 23

trends **189**.8

young people **189**.21-32

   housing rights **189**.24-5

   local authority duties **181**.26

   reasons for leaving home **189**.24, 26, 27

homeopathic hospitals **195**.18

homeopathy

arguments against **195**.25, 27

arguments for **195**.22, 32

dangers of **195**.30-31

definition **195**.24

and the NHS **195**.16-22, 24-5

10:23 campaign against **195**.31, 32

homework **139**.27, 28

homeworking scams **134**.27

homophobia **153**.13

in football **198**.25, 26

homophobic abuse **165**.13

homophobic bullying **153**.14-18; **165**.2, 9, 12-14

homosexuality **153**.1-3

causes **153**.3, 6, 7

coming out **153**.3, 8

'correction' of **153**.3

discrimination **153**.2-3, 27-8

Volume numbers appear first (in bold) followed by page numbers; a change in volume number is preceded by a semi-**colon.**

Vol. 88 Food and Nutrition

Vol. 97 Energy Matters

Vol. 99 Exploited Children

Vol. 100 Stress and Anxiety

Vol. 119 Transport Trends

Vol. 129 Gambling Trends

Vol. 134 Customers and Consumerism

Vol. 138 A Genetically Modified Future?

Vol. 139 The Education Problem

Vol. 140 Vegetarian and Vegan Diets

Vol. 141 Mental Health

Vol. 142 Media Issues

Vol. 144 The Cloning Debate

Vol. 146 Sustainability and Environment

Vol. 147 The Terrorism Problem

Vol. 148 Religious Beliefs

Vol. 149 A Classless Society?

Vol. 150 Migration and Population

Vol. 151 Climate Change

Vol. 152 Euthanasia and the Right to Die

Vol. 153 Sexual Orientation and Society

Vol. 154 The Gender Gap

Vol. 155 Domestic Abuse

Vol. 156 Travel and Tourism

Vol. 157 The Problem of Globalisation

Vol. 158 The Internet Revolution

Vol. 159 An Ageing Population

Vol. 160 Poverty and Exclusion

Vol. 161 Waste Issues

Vol. 162 Staying Fit

Vol. 163 Drugs in the UK

Vol. 164 The AIDS Crisis

Vol. 165 Bullying Issues

Vol. 166 Marriage and Cohabitation

Vol. 167 Our Human Rights

Vol. 168 Privacy and Surveillance

Vol. 169 The Animal Rights Debate

Vol. 170 Body Image and Self-Esteem

Vol. 171 Abortion – Rights and Ethics

Vol. 172 Racial and Ethnic Discrimination

Vol. 173 Sexual Health

Vol. 174 Selling Sex

Vol. 175 Citizenship and Participation

Vol. 176 Health Issues for Young People

Vol. 177 Crime in the UK

Vol. 178 Reproductive Ethics

Vol. 179 Tackling Child Abuse

Vol. 180 Money and Finances

Vol. 181 The Housing Issue

Vol. 182 Teenage Conceptions

Vol. 183 Work and Employment

Vol. 184 Understanding Eating Disorders

Vol. 185 Student Matters

Vol. 186 Cannabis Use

Vol. 187 Health and the State

Vol. 188 Tobacco and Health

Vol. 189 The Homeless Population

Vol. 190 Coping with Depression

Vol. 191 The Changing Family

Vol. 192 Bereavement and Grief

Vol. 193 Endangered Species

Vol. 194 Responsible Drinking

Vol. 195 Alternative Medicine

Vol. 196 Censorship Issues

Vol. 197 Living with Disability

Vol. 198 Sport and Society

Vol. 199 Self-Harming and Suicide

genetic factors **153.**6, 7
and the media **142.**39; **153.**23-5
and mental disorder **153.**3, 4
see also gay men; lesbians
hormone disrupting chemicals, effect on wildlife **193.**16-17
hormones
abuse in sport **198.**29-30
and depression **190.**2
hospitals
care standards **187.**4, 26-8
in 1948 **187.**7-8
post mortems **192.**31
superbugs **187.**28-9
treatment for self-harm **199.**13-14, 15
host surrogacy **178.**7, 13
hostels for homeless people **189.**17, 31-2, 35
hot water bottles, recycling **161.**24-5
hours of work
young workers **183.**28-9
House of Commons **131.**15
House of Lords **131.**15
house prices **134.**25
house size, new homes **181.**15
household crime, racial identity of victims **115.**10
household debt **180.**9
household waste **161.**1, 5, 6, 18-19, 31
composition of **161.**1
households
and energy efficiency **97.**2, 27-30, 31, 32-3; **151.**39
gender roles **154.**15, 21
financial **180.**18-19
growth in numbers of **181.**2
income inequalities **160.**6-7
minimum standard income **160.**8; **180.**6
structure and poverty **160.**2
see also families; homeless households
houses of multiple occupation **181.**19-20
housework, and gender **154.**15
housing **181.**1-39
census information **150.**36
and children **181.**9-11, 13, 14
debt **134.**23
disability rights **197.**21-2
disabled children **197.**37
expenditure **134.**4
home building **181.**2
affordable homes **181.**6, 29
green belt land **181.**21
greenfield sites **181.**22, 36
self-build **181.**30-31
housing market as economic indicator **180.**5
new homes
lack of space **181.**15
need for **181.**6, 29
political party policies **181.**23
older people **159.**4
overcrowding **181.**14
priority needs households **189.**2, 3
problems for young people **180.**35-6; **191.**26, 27
size of new houses **181.**15
and social improvement **181.**33-5

students **185.**7
young people **180.**35-6; **189.**24-5
housing associations
and self-build projects **181.**30, 31
and tenants' rights to move **181.**35-6
human-animal embryos **144.**9, 11, 13, 14, 20; **178.**35
human-ape hybrids **144.**11
human cloning **144.**1-14
ethical issues **144.**2-3, 5-6, 7-8
public attitudes **144.**35
human dignity
and cloning **144.**3
and inter-species mixing **144.**12
human embryos
stem cells *see* embryonic stem cells
hybrid embryos **144.**9, 11, 13, 14, 20
Human Fertilisation and Embryology Act **144.**15, 27; **171.**5, 7
human genes
in bacteria **144.**11
in mice **144.**11
see also hybrid embryos
human growth hormones (HGHs) and sport **198.**30
human reproductive cloning
autonomy issues **144.**3
benefits **144.**2
and dignity **144.**3
ethical concerns **144.**2-3, 8
human rights **167.**1-27
and child labour **99.**4, 6
domestic work **99.**8
and child soldiers **99.**30, 31-2
and children's rights **167.**28-39
controversies **167.**5
and corporal punishment **179.**30, 31-2
definitions **167.**1, 4
development of **167.** 1, 6-7
female migrants **150.**15
laws **167.**2
see also Human Rights Act
and politics **167.**4-5
and privacy **168.**1, 3
public attitudes to **167.**19
timeline **167.**6-7
Human Rights, Universal Declaration of **167.**8-10, 14
and privacy **168.**3
Human Rights Act **167.**3, 4, 5, 15-18
achievements **167.**17-18
costs **167.**18
failures **167.**16-17
and freedom of expression **196.**14
humanism
and abortion **171.**19-21
and animal welfare **140.**31-3
and embryo research **144.**7-8; **178.**36-7
and ethics **148.**13-16
funerals **192.**37
and the Golden Rule **148.**8, 15-16
motivation **148.**14
humidity, global increase **151.**2
hunger **160.**28

Millennium Development Goals **160**.30
hunger strikers, force-feeding **167**.26
hunting **169**.27-36
    after the ban **169**.34-5
    arguments against **169**.27, 30-33, 33
    arguments for **169**.27
    for bushmeat **193**.23
    captive animals **193**.17
    draghunting **169**.33
    endangered species **193**.1-2
    as food source **140**.17
    hunt monitors **169**.35
    hunting with dogs **169**.27-36
    increased popularity since ban **169**.34-5
    law on (Hunting Act 2004) **169**.28-9, 30-32
    public attitudes to **169**.29, 36
    trail hunting **169**.34
Huntingdon's disease **141**.6-7
hybrid animals **144**.10-12
hybrid embryos **144**.9, 11, 13, 14, 20
hybrid vehicles **119**.22
hybridisation **138**.12-13
    see also cross-contamination; cross-pollination
hydrocarbon (HC) emissions **119**.15
hypertension *see* high blood pressure
hypnosis **195**.4
hypomania **190**.9

ICSI (intracytoplasmic sperm injection) **178**.8
identity
    British identity of non-white ethnic groups **115**.38
    identity confusion **149**.4-5
    protection in interviews **142**.12
    protection online **158**.10
    racial, victims of crime **115**.10
    religious **115**.5, 26
    and social class **149**.3, 4, 18, 19, 24
    social identity and football supporters **141**.32-3
identity (ID) cards **131**.13-14; **168**.14-19

    benefits **168**.14-16
    costs **168**.17, 18-19
    problems **168**.17-19
    public attitudes to **168**.16
identity disorders **141**.11
identity fraud **134**.27-8, 28-9; **158**.3, 32, 33-4
    and ID cards **168**.14-15, 18
    statistics **168**.15-16
illegal broadcasting **142**.7
illegal immigrants
    attitudes to **150**.3
    and National Identity Scheme **168**.16, 18
illegal planting of GM crops **138**.19
illegal wildlife trade souvenirs **156**.32
images, effects on young people's smoking **188**.24-6
IMF (International Monetary Fund) **157**.6, 10, 17
immigration
    attitudes to **150**.3, 13-14, 17, 18-19
    church attendance of immigrants **148**.23-4
    definition **150**.21
    lack of accurate data **150**.19
    and globalisation **157**.37
    and population growth, UK **150**.16
    problems of **150**.16-17
    quota system proposal **131**.10
    and social housing **181**.12
    statistics, UK **150**.4, 8-9
    worldwide **150**.33
immune system
    and complementary therapies **195**.7
    and HIV **164**.1
imports
    indecent articles **196**.23
    UK dependence on **146**.4-6
imprisonment *see* prison
in vitro fertilisation (IVF) **178**.1, 5-8, 11
    errors **178**.22
    ethical dilemmas **178**.17
    international comparisons **178**.8
    and multiple births **178**.6-7, 21-2
    and older mothers **178**.17, 19-20
    statistics **178**.5-6

Volume numbers appear first (in bold) followed by page numbers; a change in volume number is preceded by a semi-**colon.**

Vol. 88 Food and Nutrition
Vol. 97 Energy Matters
Vol. 99 Exploited Children
Vol. 100 Stress and Anxiety
Vol. 119 Transport Trends
Vol. 129 Gambling Trends
Vol. 134 Customers and Consumerism
Vol. 138 A Genetically Modified Future?
Vol. 139 The Education Problem
Vol. 140 Vegetarian and Vegan Diets
Vol. 141 Mental Health
Vol. 142 Media Issues
Vol. 144 The Cloning Debate
Vol. 146 Sustainability and Environment
Vol. 147 The Terrorism Problem
Vol. 148 Religious Beliefs
Vol. 149 A Classless Society?
Vol. 150 Migration and Population
Vol. 151 Climate Change
Vol. 152 Euthanasia and the Right to Die
Vol. 153 Sexual Orientation and Society
Vol. 154 The Gender Gap
Vol. 155 Domestic Abuse

Vol. 156 Travel and Tourism
Vol. 157 The Problem of Globalisation
Vol. 158 The Internet Revolution
Vol. 159 An Ageing Population
Vol. 160 Poverty and Exclusion
Vol. 161 Waste Issues
Vol. 162 Staying Fit
Vol. 163 Drugs in the UK
Vol. 164 The AIDS Crisis
Vol. 165 Bullying Issues
Vol. 166 Marriage and Cohabitation
Vol. 167 Our Human Rights
Vol. 168 Privacy and Surveillance
Vol. 169 The Animal Rights Debate
Vol. 170 Body Image and Self-Esteem
Vol. 171 Abortion – Rights and Ethics
Vol. 172 Racial and Ethnic Discrimination
Vol. 173 Sexual Health
Vol. 174 Selling Sex
Vol. 175 Citizenship and Participation
Vol. 176 Health Issues for Young People
Vol. 177 Crime in the UK
Vol. 178 Reproductive Ethics

Vol. 179 Tackling Child Abuse
Vol. 180 Money and Finances
Vol. 181 The Housing Issue
Vol. 182 Teenage Conceptions
Vol. 183 Work and Employment
Vol. 184 Understanding Eating Disorders
Vol. 185 Student Matters
Vol. 186 Cannabis Use
Vol. 187 Health and the State
Vol. 188 Tobacco and Health
Vol. 189 The Homeless Population
Vol. 190 Coping with Depression
Vol. 191 The Changing Family
Vol. 192 Bereavement and Grief
Vol. 193 Endangered Species
Vol. 194 Responsible Drinking
Vol. 195 Alternative Medicine
Vol. 196 Censorship Issues
Vol. 197 Living with Disability
Vol. 198 Sport and Society
Vol. 199 Self-Harming and Suicide

tagging embryos **178**.22-3
travelling abroad for **178**.18, 20
inactivity
children **162**.13, 15, 25
health effects **162**.11
incentives
for health care **187**.37
for reducing waste **161**.38
for weight loss **162**.22-3
incineration of waste **161**.7
incitement to religious hatred **148**.29
inclusion
disabled children **197**.36-7
education **197**.15, 27, 37
and sport **198**.18-26
in the workforce **183**.26-7
incomes
and children's educational attainment **149**.25
effect on children's character **191**.6
global **157**.2
inequalities **160**.6, 7
minimum standard **160**.8; **180**.6
minimum wage. young people **183**.28
pensioners **159**.3
and social class **149**.19, 20
social housing tenants **181**.35
stress and income levels **100**.13
and voter turnout **131**.19
incontinence
sufferers **159**.4
and stem cell therapy **144**.21
indecency **196**.22-3
independent schools
and university applications **185**.19
India
censorship of sexual content on the Internet **196**.37
street children as tourist attraction **156**.33-4
indigenous people and poverty **160**.25
indirect discrimination
racial **115**.7, 11
on sexuality **153**.38
Indonesia
human rights abuses **167**.13
palm oil industry and biodiversity **193**.8-9
indoor (contained) GMOs **138**.12
induced pluripotent stem cells (iPS cells) **178**.38
industry
and child labour **99**.1, 2
costs of smoking **188**.22-3
motivations for GM development **138**.8
inequality
attitudes to **160**.9
children **167**.35
in climate change effects **151**.11, 19
in employment **183**.13
effect of free trade **157**.13, 23-4
gender *see* gender gap
global **160**.26, 28
and globalisation **157**.2, 3-4, 9
of incomes **160**.6, 7
of global resource usage **193**.4

and segregation **115**.30, 31, 32
and tourism **156**.20
infertility **178**.2-5
information
as consumer right **134**.1-2
and ethical consumerism **134**.33-4
patients' rights **187**.14
personal, control of **158**.31-4; **168**.10-11, 31-2, 37
privacy **168**.2
and the web **158**.2
information technology (IT)
benefits **157**.1
and globalisation **157**.1, 2, 15
inheritance and cohabitation **166**.15
injuries
from domestic violence **155**.30
young people **176**.4
insects
declining numbers **193**.26
bees and pollinators **193**.27-8
GM viral infections **138**.13-14
role in ecosystems **193**.26
stag beetles, London **193**.35
insomnia and stress **100**.19, 29
insulin and sports drug abuse **198**.30, 35
institutional elements of marriage **166**.2-3
institutions, leaving
as cause of homelessness **189**.6
and help with housing **189**.25
instructions to discriminate **115**.12
insulation, home **151**.38, 39
insurance
car insurance offences **119**.9
and home buying **181**.24
integrated healthcare **195**.23
intellectual property rights *see* patents
intelligent design **148**.37-9
intelligent transport systems **119**.38
intensive farming
arguments for **169**.11-12
chickens **169**.13
see also battery eggs
interactive gambling **129**.17-26
interdependence, global **146**.4-6
interest-only mortgages **181**.28
interest rates
annual percentage rate (APR) **180**.26
as economic indicator **180**5
inter-ethnic marriages **115**.25
see also mixed-race relationships
interfaith relations, young people **148**.32-3
intergender **153**.13
international companies *see* multinational corporations
International Monetary Fund (IMF) *see* IMF
international parental chid abduction **166**.36
international students **139**.30, 31, 32
and terrorism **147**.13-14
international terrorism, history of **147**.4-5
international trade **157**.17-39
ecologically wasteful **146**.5
facts **157**.19

and genetic modification **138**.27
and poverty **157**.26-7; **160**.37-8
and taxes **157**.12-13
UK dependence on **146**.4-6
see also free trade; globalisation
Internet
   abortion drugs availability **171**.35-6
   addiction **142**.37; **158**.38-9
   advertising **158**.5
   anti-extremism projects **147**.34
   banking **180**.14
   broadband access **158**.5-6, 17, 18
   bullying by e-mail **165**.23-4, 38-9
   and censorship **196**.27-39
     China **158**.37; **196**.27-8, 30
   and child sex abuse **179**.15-17; **196**.39
   and children and young people **158**.20-21
     viewing pornography **196**.38
   development of **158**.1
   downloading **158**.33, 35-6
   and entertainment **158**.21-2
   family usage **158**.7-8
   filesharing **158**.36
   fraud **134**.26-9
   future of **158**.25-6
   gambling *see* online gambling
   and globalisation **157**.1, 2, 15
   herbal medicine purchasing **195**.8, 39
   influence on young people smoking **188**.26
   journalism register **142**.16
   and media regulation **142**.2
   memorial websites **192**.38-9
   National Lottery games, and under 16s **129**.12-13
   as news source **142**.33
   and newspapers **142**.9
   and older people **158**.4
   online activity **158**.4, 15
     children **158**.20-21
     older people **158**.4
     young people **158**.27
   online bullying *see* cyberbullying
   phishing **134**.27-8, 28-9; **158**.33-4

   and privacy **168**.34-6
   pro-eating disorder websites **184**.25-7
   reaching capacity **158**.24
   regulation **142**.2
   risks **158**.27-39
   safety **165**.26-7, 30-31
     and National Identity Scheme **168**.15
    social networking sites **179**.18
   and self-harm **199**.19
   and the sexual exploitation of children **99**.16, 21, 24
   shopping **158**.3, 30-31
     Europe **134**.15-16
     and gender **134**.16
   social networking sites **142**.35, 36, 38; **157**.15; **168**.34-6
     safety **179**.18
   support for suicidal people **199**.33, 35
   surveillance **168**.8, 13-14, 32-3
   and terrorism **147**.8-9
   and travel industry **156**.1, 13, 14
   trends **158**.1-26
   see also child pornography; e-mail; safety and the Internet; websites
intersexuality **153**.13
inter-species mixing **144**.10-12
intestacy rules **192**.25-6
intracytoplasmic sperm injection (ICSI) **178**.8
invertebrates, conservation needs **193**.26
investment in stock market **180**.7
investment scams **134**.27
involuntary euthanasia **152**.1
involuntary smoking *see* passive smoking
iodine and vegetarian diet **140**.3
iPS cells (induced pluripotent stem cells) **178**.38
IQ **197**.6
   and gender **154**.24
   and post traumatic stress disorder **141**.3
   and vegetarian diet **140**.10
Iran
   demonstrations via the Internet **196**.32
   government control of the Internet **196**.33
Ireland, Northern
   abortion law **171**.15-16

Volume numbers appear first (in bold) followed by page numbers; a change in volume number is preceded by a semi-**colon.**

Vol. 88 Food and Nutrition
Vol. 97 Energy Matters
Vol. 99 Exploited Children
Vol. 100 Stress and Anxiety
Vol. 119 Transport Trends
Vol. 129 Gambling Trends
Vol. 134 Customers and Consumerism
Vol. 138 A Genetically Modified Future?
Vol. 139 The Education Problem
Vol. 140 Vegetarian and Vegan Diets
Vol. 141 Mental Health
Vol. 142 Media Issues
Vol. 144 The Cloning Debate
Vol. 146 Sustainability and Environment
Vol. 147 The Terrorism Problem
Vol. 148 Religious Beliefs
Vol. 149 A Classless Society?
Vol. 150 Migration and Population
Vol. 151 Climate Change
Vol. 152 Euthanasia and the Right to Die
Vol. 153 Sexual Orientation and Society
Vol. 154 The Gender Gap
Vol. 155 Domestic Abuse

Vol. 156 Travel and Tourism
Vol. 157 The Problem of Globalisation
Vol. 158 The Internet Revolution
Vol. 159 An Ageing Population
Vol. 160 Poverty and Exclusion
Vol. 161 Waste Issues
Vol. 162 Staying Fit
Vol. 163 Drugs in the UK
Vol. 164 The AIDS Crisis
Vol. 165 Bullying Issues
Vol. 166 Marriage and Cohabitation
Vol. 167 Our Human Rights
Vol. 168 Privacy and Surveillance
Vol. 169 The Animal Rights Debate
Vol. 170 Body Image and Self-Esteem
Vol. 171 Abortion – Rights and Ethics
Vol. 172 Racial and Ethnic Discrimination
Vol. 173 Sexual Health
Vol. 174 Selling Sex
Vol. 175 Citizenship and Participation
Vol. 176 Health Issues for Young People
Vol. 177 Crime in the UK
Vol. 178 Reproductive Ethics

Vol. 179 Tackling Child Abuse
Vol. 180 Money and Finances
Vol. 181 The Housing Issue
Vol. 182 Teenage Conceptions
Vol. 183 Work and Employment
Vol. 184 Understanding Eating Disorders
Vol. 185 Student Matters
Vol. 186 Cannabis Use
Vol. 187 Health and the State
Vol. 188 Tobacco and Health
Vol. 189 The Homeless Population
Vol. 190 Coping with Depression
Vol. 191 The Changing Family
Vol. 192 Bereavement and Grief
Vol. 193 Endangered Species
Vol. 194 Responsible Drinking
Vol. 195 Alternative Medicine
Vol. 196 Censorship Issues
Vol. 197 Living with Disability
Vol. 198 Sport and Society
Vol. 199 Self-Harming and Suicide

homelessness **189**.4
iron in the diet **88**.6, 15
  red meat **140**.12
  sources **140**.4, 7; **176**.8
  teenagers' needs **176**.8
  and vegetarian diet **140**.1, 3, 7
Islam **148**.3-4
  and anti-extremism **147**.34
  and the census **148**.7
  and faith schools **148**.35
  festivals **148**.3
  food rules **148**.3-4; 11
  fundamentalist beliefs of young Muslims **147**.16-17
  funerals **192**.34-5
  mosque governance standards **147**.34
  observance trends, Britain **148**.18-19
  preventing youth extremism **148**.30-31
  public perceptions of **147**.26
  teaching in British Mosques **147**.17-18
  and terrorism **147**.15, 26-7
  see also Muslims
Islamic mortgages **181**.28
Islamophobia **115**.36
  and national identity **131**.11
isolation, older people **159**.3, 8, 17, 30
ITV and portrayals of homosexuality **153**.24-5
IVF *see* in vitro fertilisation
ivory trade **193**.2, 19

J

Japan, religious observance **148**.24
jewellery, recycling **161**.24
Jews (Judaism) **148**.4-5
  and the Census (2001) **148**.7
  and faith schools **148**.35
  food rules **148**.4, 10-11
  funerals **192**.34-5
  and racism laws **115**.26
jihad **147**.15
Jobcentre Plus, Disability Symbol **197**.26-7
jobs
  distribution inequalities **149**.28
  job satisfaction **154**.18; **183**.3-6
Jobseekers Allowance **100**.23
journalists
  and libel law **142**.27
  protection of sources **142**.22
  regulation **142**.16
  talking to **142**.11-14
journey length trends **119**.29
  travelling to school **119**.30
junk mail **134**.26, 28; **161**.19, 26
justice system and gender equality **154**.4
juvenile arthritis **197**.16-17

K

ketamine **163**.18-20; **194**.9-10

Key Stages (schools) **139**.1-2, 5
Klebsiella (hospital superbug) **187**.28
knee repair, stem cell therapy **144**.21
knife crime **177**.15-16, 29-30
  sentencing **177**.38-9
  statistics **177**.38, 39
  young people's concerns **177**.15-16
knives and the law **177**.7
knowledge, globalisation of **157**.1
Kyoto Protocol **151**.2
  Clean Development Mechanism **151**.17
  Kyoto Compliant emission reduction projects **151**.21
  UK target **146**.8

L

labelling
  ethical products **134**.34
  GM animal feed **138**.25
  GM food **138**.11, 39
  products **134**.1-2
labour market, UK **183**.16-17
labour migration **150**.1-2
  see also migrant workers
lacto-ovo-vegetarians **140**.2
lacto-vegetarians **140**.2
lactose, and vegetarians **140**.19
lads' magazines **142**.29
  and body image **170**.28
landfill **146**.23; 1-2, 6-7, 10
  hazardous waste **161**.32
  restoring sites to green space **161**.33
  tax **161**.12, 20, 35
landlords
  duties to disabled people **197**.22
  reluctant **181**.17
  and tenants' rights **181**.16
language
  in advertising **134**.9
  and disability
    offensive language **197**.28-9; **196**.24
    preferred terminology **197**.27
  offensive language on television **196**.21, 24
  of technology **158**.16-17
lanolin, and vegetarians **140**.19
law *see* legislation
law and drugs **163**.1-2, 31-9
law-making process **131**.24
  citizen involvement **131**.25
Lawrence Report (Macpherson Inquiry) **115**.8
lead pollution **146**.36
learning, effects of cannabis **186**.9-10
learning disabilities **197**.6-7, 39
  and bullying **165**.2, 14-16, 17
  causes **197**.7
  definitions **197**.6-7, 39
  and education **197**.14-15
  and healthcare **197**.38-9
  statistics **197**.7
leaving home

after domestic abuse **155**.4-5, 6-7, 12-13, 27-8
   young people **181**.26
left-wing terrorism **147**.1
legal advice on arrest **177**.35
legal rights
   NHS patients **187**.32-3
   young workers **183**.28-9
legalising drugs, potential results **163**.39
legislation
   and abortion **171**.1, 5-7; 11-12; 15-16
      and doctors **171**.27-8
      and religion **171**.18
   age discrimination **159**.10, 11
   and alcohol
      drink-driving **194**.31, 32
      24-hour drinking **194**.20, 21
   animal experiments **169**.14, 20, 23
   animal welfare **169**.3, 4
   and assisted suicide **199**.37-8
   and begging **189**.20
   and bullying
      cyberbullying **165**.25, 39
      workplace bullying **165**.33
   and cannabis **186**.1-2, 4-5, 8, 9, 30-39
   Civil Partnership Act **153**.26-8
   on climate change **151**.17
   Communications Act and media mergers **142**.4
   and corporal punishment **167**.26-8
      European countries **179**.31
   and domestic violence **155**.2; 28; 37-8
   and drugs **163**.1-2, 33; **176**.19
   on embryo research **144**.15, 17, 27-8
   employment of young people **180**.20
   Equality Act **153**.35; **183**.13
   and euthanasia **152**.1, 16-18, 29-30
      Australia **152**.19
      Belgium **152**.4, 18, 19
      Italy **152**.10-11
      Netherlands **152**.4, 18, 19
      Scotland **152**.17, 29, 30
      Switzerland **152**.18, 19
      US, Oregon state **152**.4, 18, 19, 31, 33

and film classification **196**.14
on food additives **88**.39
on food labelling **88**.23, 24, 25
and forced marriages **155**.17
Freedom of Information Act **142**.17-21
on gambling
   Gambling Act **129**.5, 17, 23
   and gambling at work **129**.23
   online gambling **129**.17
on gender discrimination **154**.14
and HIV transmission **164**.14
and homelessness **189**.1-2, 34
human rights **167**.2
hunting with dogs **169**.27-9, 30-32
law-making process **131**.24
   citizen involvement **131**.25
libel and journalistic freedom **142**.27
libel and slander **142**.26
Poor Laws **149**.13
on privacy **168**.2-3
and racism **115**.2, 7-8, 26
   at work **115**.11-12
on religious hatred **115**.26
and sex **176**.21-2
Sexual Orientation Regulation **153**.35, 36, 37
and sexuality **153**.26-39
and smoking, children **176**.13
and squatting **181**.20
and suicide **199**.27
and sunbeds **176**.11
on surveillance **168**.10
and tenants' rights **181**.16
and weapons **177**.7, 30
leisure activities
   effect of poverty **160**.2
   older people **159**.3, 8
lesbians
   definition **153**.1
   having children **153**.20-22, 33-4; **178**.9-10
   and the media **142**.39
   see also gay couples; homosexuality
leukaemia, stem cell therapy **144**.21

Volume numbers appear first (in bold) followed by page numbers; a change in volume number is preceded by a semi-**colon.**

Vol. 88 Food and Nutrition
Vol. 97 Energy Matters
Vol. 99 Exploited Children
Vol. 100 Stress and Anxiety
Vol. 119 Transport Trends
Vol. 129 Gambling Trends
Vol. 134 Customers and Consumerism
Vol. 138 A Genetically Modified Future?
Vol. 139 The Education Problem
Vol. 140 Vegetarian and Vegan Diets
Vol. 141 Mental Health
Vol. 142 Media Issues
Vol. 144 The Cloning Debate
Vol. 146 Sustainability and Environment
Vol. 147 The Terrorism Problem
Vol. 148 Religious Beliefs
Vol. 149 A Classless Society?
Vol. 150 Migration and Population
Vol. 151 Climate Change
Vol. 152 Euthanasia and the Right to Die
Vol. 153 Sexual Orientation and Society
Vol. 154 The Gender Gap
Vol. 155 Domestic Abuse

Vol. 156 Travel and Tourism
Vol. 157 The Problem of Globalisation
Vol. 158 The Internet Revolution
Vol. 159 An Ageing Population
Vol. 160 Poverty and Exclusion
Vol. 161 Waste Issues
Vol. 162 Staying Fit
Vol. 163 Drugs in the UK
Vol. 164 The AIDS Crisis
Vol. 165 Bullying Issues
Vol. 166 Marriage and Cohabitation
Vol. 167 Our Human Rights
Vol. 168 Privacy and Surveillance
Vol. 169 The Animal Rights Debate
Vol. 170 Body Image and Self-Esteem
Vol. 171 Abortion – Rights and Ethics
Vol. 172 Racial and Ethnic Discrimination
Vol. 173 Sexual Health
Vol. 174 Selling Sex
Vol. 175 Citizenship and Participation
Vol. 176 Health Issues for Young People
Vol. 177 Crime in the UK
Vol. 178 Reproductive Ethics

Vol. 179 Tackling Child Abuse
Vol. 180 Money and Finances
Vol. 181 The Housing Issue
Vol. 182 Teenage Conceptions
Vol. 183 Work and Employment
Vol. 184 Understanding Eating Disorders
Vol. 185 Student Matters
Vol. 186 Cannabis Use
Vol. 187 Health and the State
Vol. 188 Tobacco and Health
Vol. 189 The Homeless Population
Vol. 190 Coping with Depression
Vol. 191 The Changing Family
Vol. 192 Bereavement and Grief
Vol. 193 Endangered Species
Vol. 194 Responsible Drinking
Vol. 195 Alternative Medicine
Vol. 196 Censorship Issues
Vol. 197 Living with Disability
Vol. 198 Sport and Society
Vol. 199 Self-Harming and Suicide

liability for racism at work **115**.12
libel **142**.26
    and journalism **142**.27
liberalisation **157**.12, 20
    see also free trade
licence fee, BBC **142**.6
licensing
    gambling **129**.5, 8, 23
    herbal medicines **195**.4, 37-8
    hybrid embryo research **144**.14
    stem cell research **144**.17, 27-8
licensing hours
    24-hour licensing **194**.20
    and crime **194**.21
life expectancy **150**.32, 35; **159**.6
    and obesity **176**.7
    HIV patients **164**.8-9
    and poverty **160**.38
    and smoking **188**.18
    and social class **149**.15; **188**.18
    ways of increasing **159**.32-4
    UK **159**.3, 34
life insurance cover and home buying **181**.24
life stages and social identity **149**.23
lifestyle
    and ageing **159**.2, 34
    and depression **190**.3
    and life expectancy **159**.33-4
    stress and changes in **100**.19
    and weight loss **162**.20
lifetime debt **180**.11-12
light bulbs, recycling **161**.24
light therapy for Seasonal Affective Disorder **141**.35; **190**.6-7
listeria **88**.28-9
literacy
    employees' literacy problems **139**.17
    and poverty **160**.28
litter **161**.15-16, 21
liver damage
    and alcohol **194**.6
    and stem cell therapy **144**.22
living funerals **192**.36
living wills *see* advance directives (living wills)
LL601 rice **138**.31-4
loans **180**.27
    student **139**.34; **180**.28, 33; **185**.2
    see also credit; debt
local authorities
    duty to house **189**.1-2, 34
    and greenfield development **181**.22
    and housing young people **181**.26-7
    and self-build projects **181**.30
    and social housing **181**.29
    and surveillance **168**.20-21
    and tourism **156**.9
    see also council tenants
local communities, effects of tourism **156**.22
lodgers' rights **181**.16
logging
    destructive **146**.30

effect on wildlife **193**.4
London
    bombings
        and faith hate crime **115**.27
        impact on Muslims **115**.36
    congestion charging **119**.12, 38
    counter-terrorism measures **147**.31
    hostels for homeless people **189**.35
    illegal radio stations **142**.7
    and migrant workers **150**.11
    multicultural tolerance **115**.23
    Olympics and tourism **156**.13
    rare wildlife species **193**.35
    rough sleepers **189**.16
    underground travel, disabled people **197**.12
lone parents
    children of **191**.12
    and the recession **191**.13
    statistics **166**.4, 15; **191**.1, 12
    working mothers **191**.36
loneliness
    after divorce **166**.23
    older people **159**.3, 8, 17, 30
long-term illness **159**.4
lotteries **129**.2
    scams **134**.26
    see also National Lottery
low carbon technologies **97**.4
low-cost home ownership **181**.25
low income families
    subsidised broadband access **158**.18
low income workers **160**.5
low self-esteem **170**.2, 3
    and bullying **165**.16
    causes of **170**.8
low-tar cigarettes **188**.7, 10
LPG vehicles **119**.20
LSD **163**.6
lung cancer
    and cannabis use **186**.15, 16
    and smoking, **188**.6, 8
lung damage
    through cannabis use **186**.28
    through smoking **188**.5

M

Macpherson Inquiry (Lawrence Report) **115**.8
macrobiotic diets **140**.2; **195**.4-5
magazines
    influence on body image **170**.28
    influence on young people smoking **188**.25-6
    and sex education **142**.28, 29
magic mushrooms **163**.6
major (clinical) depression **190**.2, 21
malaria, Millennium Development Goals **160**.32
male stereotyping as barrier to university entrance **139**.38
male violence, attitudes to **177**.5
malignant melanoma **176**.10-11
malnutrition **176**.4

managers
    gender gap **154**.17
    gender pay gap **154**.38
    and workplace stress **100**.18, 25
mandatory eviction **181**.16
mania **190**.8, 21
manic depression *see* bipolar affective disorder
MAOIs (monoamine oxidase inhibitors) **190**.11, 33
marijuana *see* herbal cannabis
marine ecosystems, effect of climate change **151**.9
marital status
    and health **166**.15
    and smoking **188**.1
marker-assisted selection (MAS) **138**.37-9
marker genes **138**.4
market size, gambling industry **129**.4
    National Lottery **129**.9, 10
    online gambling **129**.17, 19
marriage **166**.1-20
    age at **166**.4, 6
    arranged marriages **166**.16
    attitudes to **166**.1-2, 7, 9-11
    and Civil Partnerships **153**.26
    'common law' marriage **166**.12
    expectations of cohabiting partners **166**.2, 7
    financial incentives **166**.5; **191**.2
    forced marriages **155**.16-18; **166**.17-20
    and HIV/AIDS **96**.24-5, 29, 34, 35
    institutional elements **166**.2-3
    inter-ethnic **115**.25
    male and female attitudes to **166**.3
    reasons for marrying **166**.2
    reasons for not marrying **166**.2, 9-11
    relational elements **166**.2-3
    statistics **166**.4, 6; **191**.1, 3
    trends **191**.1-4
    unhappy **166**.7-8
mass surveillance **168**.6
maternal health, Millennium Development Goals **160**.31-2
maternal mortality **154**.12
maternity leave **183**.18, 21, 23, 24; **191**.37-8
    effect on businesses **183**.23

maternity pay **191**.38
maternity rights **191**.37-8
mathematics, A-level performance **139**.18
mature students **139**.30, 32
MBCT (mindfulness-based cognitive therapy) **190**.34-6
MDMA *see* ecstasy
means-tested benefits **160**.23, 24
meat consumption **88**.6, 26, 31; **140**.12-13, 15-18
    alternatives to meat **140**.19, 26
    bushmeat trade **193**.23
    effects **140**.13
    and fat **140**.12
    game as food source **140**.15, 17
    health issues **140**.13, 21, 30
    illegal meat **88**.39
    nutrients **140**.12, 14
meat production
    and animal welfare **169**.10
    effects of **140**.13, 16-17
    free range **169**.11-12
    intensively farmed chickens **169**.13
    organic **140**.29-30
medical model of disability **197**.2
media
    accountability **142**.17-30
    and body image **170**.22, 23, 24, 28, 30-31, 38; **184**.23-4
        men **184**.13
    breaking ethnic stereotypes **115**.22
    complaints *see* Press Complaints Commission; Ofcom
    control **142**.1-16
    convergence **142**.1-2
    drug death reporting **186**.32-3
    and homosexuality **153**.23-5
    impact **142**.31-9
    influence on young people smoking **188**.25-6
    intrusion **142**.23, 25, 26
    mergers **142**.4
    over-reaction to terrorism **147**.10-11
    and the permissive society **196**.25-6
    press freedom **196**.1-2
    press regulation, public opinion **196**.6
    and privacy **168**.7, 28-9

Volume numbers appear first (in bold) followed by page numbers; a change in volume number is preceded by a semi-**colon**.

Vol. 88 Food and Nutrition
Vol. 97 Energy Matters
Vol. 99 Exploited Children
Vol. 100 Stress and Anxiety
Vol. 119 Transport Trends
Vol. 129 Gambling Trends
Vol. 134 Customers and Consumerism
Vol. 138 A Genetically Modified Future?
Vol. 139 The Education Problem
Vol. 140 Vegetarian and Vegan Diets
Vol. 141 Mental Health
Vol. 142 Media Issues
Vol. 144 The Cloning Debate
Vol. 146 Sustainability and Environment
Vol. 147 The Terrorism Problem
Vol. 148 Religious Beliefs
Vol. 149 A Classless Society?
Vol. 150 Migration and Population
Vol. 151 Climate Change
Vol. 152 Euthanasia and the Right to Die
Vol. 153 Sexual Orientation and Society
Vol. 154 The Gender Gap
Vol. 155 Domestic Abuse

Vol. 156 Travel and Tourism
Vol. 157 The Problem of Globalisation
Vol. 158 The Internet Revolution
Vol. 159 An Ageing Population
Vol. 160 Poverty and Exclusion
Vol. 161 Waste Issues
Vol. 162 Staying Fit
Vol. 163 Drugs in the UK
Vol. 164 The AIDS Crisis
Vol. 165 Bullying Issues
Vol. 166 Marriage and Cohabitation
Vol. 167 Our Human Rights
Vol. 168 Privacy and Surveillance
Vol. 169 The Animal Rights Debate
Vol. 170 Body Image and Self-Esteem
Vol. 171 Abortion – Rights and Ethics
Vol. 172 Racial and Ethnic Discrimination
Vol. 173 Sexual Health
Vol. 174 Selling Sex
Vol. 175 Citizenship and Participation
Vol. 176 Health Issues for Young People
Vol. 177 Crime in the UK
Vol. 178 Reproductive Ethics

Vol. 179 Tackling Child Abuse
Vol. 180 Money and Finances
Vol. 181 The Housing Issue
Vol. 182 Teenage Conceptions
Vol. 183 Work and Employment
Vol. 184 Understanding Eating Disorders
Vol. 185 Student Matters
Vol. 186 Cannabis Use
Vol. 187 Health and the State
Vol. 188 Tobacco and Health
Vol. 189 The Homeless Population
Vol. 190 Coping with Depression
Vol. 191 The Changing Family
Vol. 192 Bereavement and Grief
Vol. 193 Endangered Species
Vol. 194 Responsible Drinking
Vol. 195 Alternative Medicine
Vol. 196 Censorship Issues
Vol. 197 Living with Disability
Vol. 198 Sport and Society
Vol. 199 Self-Harming and Suicide

and public perception of crime **177**.3-4

and suicide **199**.35, 36

teenage magazines **142**.28

women in the media **154**.11

see also broadcasting; films; Internet; newspapers; radio; television

mediation and divorce **166**.26, 35, 38-9

medical abortion ('the abortion pill') **171**.2, 35, 36

medical benefits, GM crops **138**.9-10

see also pharming

medical insurance **187**.24

medical model of disability **197**.2

medical profession

attitudes to abortion **171**.25-8, 34

attitudes to euthanasia **152**.7, 8, 24-6, 27-8

effects of legalizing euthanasia **152**.7

see also doctors

medical research and animal experimentation **140**.32-3; **144**.34

medical tourism **156**.4-5

medical treatment

and the Mental Capacity Act **152**.37, 38

for obesity **162**.2-3, 6

patient's right to refuse **152**.2, 10-11

premature babies **152**.4, 32, 34

withdrawing or withholding **152**.3, 5-6

see also palliative care

medical waste disposal **161**.24

medically-assisted dying *see* physician-assisted suicide

medicinal drug use **163**.1

cannabis **186**.8, 16-17

medicines

assessment for NHS use **187**.22-3

buying **195**.8

online buying of herbal medicines **195**.8, 39

effects on fertility **178**.4, 5

from GM crops (pharming) **138**.4, 9-10, 20-22

meditation as treatment for depression **190**.34-6; **195**.15

melanoma **176**.10-11

memorial websites **192**.38-9

men

and alcohol limits **194**.14

attitudes **154**.16

body image and lads' magazines **170**.28

and compulsive shopping **134**.14

and domestic violence **155**.12-13

and eating disorders **184**.11-12, 13, 20

fertility problems **178**.3, 4-5, 8

gender stereotypes **154**.7-8

and household financial roles **180**.18-19

marriage expectations **166**.3

and mental health problems **141**.1; **190**.18-19

and online shopping **134**.16

parenting roles **191**.30-33

paternity rights **191**.39

post-natal depression **190**.16-17

and sexual health **96**.13

and smoking **188**.1, 15

and stress **100**.13, 19

and suicide **199**.21, 28

Mental Capacity Act

and advance directives **152**.37

and doctors' right to end life **152**.38

mental health **141**.2, 34-6; **176**.4, 29-39

and abortion **171**.9-10, 33

and alcohol **194**.6

awareness of **176**.31-2

benefits of exercise **141**.34, 39; **162**.37, 38

and cannabis **163**.35; **186**.10-13, 16, 28-9, 30, 31, 32

children **141**.37; **176**.29-30; 36-7

and diet **141**.30-31, 34

and domestic violence **155**.5

education in **141**.37

and homeless people **189**.9-11

and older people **159**.4

see also dementia

risk factors **176**.29

statistics, young people **190**.27

students **185**.8

and terrorism threat **147**.12

treatment **176**.30

and workplace stress **100**.17-18, 20

young people **176**.4, 29-39; **190**.27

see also dementia; depression

Mental Health Act 2007 **141**.26

'nearest relative' powers **190**.11

mental health trusts **187**.6

mental illness

attitudes to **141**.25, 27

and cannabis **163**.35

children **141**.1, 20-21

and criminal behaviour **141**.2, 22

definition **141**.1

genetic predisposition to **141**.24

help for people with **141**.34-6

and homosexuality **153**.3, 6

and poverty **141**.2, 22

prevalence **141**.1

and self-harm **199**.2

and suicide **199**.21, 24

see also depression; schizophrenia

mercy killing (non-voluntary euthanasia) **152**.1, 3

metabolism **88**.15

metals recycling **161**.24

aluminium **161**.22, 27

methamphetamine (crystal meth) **163**.16-17, 32

methane

emissions from agriculture **151**.7

trapping **151**.36

MI5 (Security Service) **147**.2

MI6 (Secret Intelligence Service) **147**.2

mice

and creation of embryonic stem cells **144**.26

with human gene material **144**.11

microbes **88**.27, 28-9

microbicides **96**.34, 35

microgeneration of energy **151**.39

middle-classes **149**.19-20

residential mobility **149**.26

and university application discrimination **149**.7

mifepristone (the abortion pill) **171**.2

migrant workers

exploitation **150**.14, 15, 19, 20, 22
    need for **150**.11
    and slavery **167**.21
    UK **150**.4-5
migrants
    attitudes to **150**.3, 13-14, 17, 18-19
    and crime **150**.12, 13
    definition **150**.21
    and economic growth **150**.11, 17
    and sexual health **150**.21-3
migration **150**.1-27, 35
    data collection **150**.5
    definition **150**.4, 21
    effect on environment **150**.26-7
    global trends **150**.1-2
    lack of accurate data **150**.6, 19, 23
    reasons for **150**.21, 24-5
    statistics **150**.4, 8-9, 23, 26, 35
    and unemployment **150**.9-10
military globalisation **157**.2
milk
    from cloned cows **144**.36-8, 39
    vegetarian alternatives **140**.22, 26
Millennium Development Goals **160**.26, 28, 20-32
    and gender discrimination **154**.14
    and sustainable development **146**.1-2
mindfulness-based cognitive therapy (MBCT) **190**.34-6
minerals and vegetarian diets **140**.3
minimum income standard **160**.8; **180**.6
minimum pricing, alcohol **194**.36, 37
minimum wage, young workers **183**.28
ministers of religion **148**.1
minority ethnic groups *see* ethnic minorities
mitochondrial DNA **144**.17
mixed-faith relationships **115**.39
mixed-race people, Britain **115**.24-5
    as victims of crime **115**.10
mixed-race relationships **115**.22-3, 24-5
MNCs *see* (multi-national corporations)
mobile phones
    bullying by **165**.23
    concerns about **158**.12, 32

    and gambling **129**.18, 26
    household ownership **134**.5
    information logging **168**.8
    and social networking **158**.11-12
    usage trends **158**.4-5; 11-14
models of disability **197**.2
Muhammed, Danish cartoons of **142**.34
money
    attitudes to, and social class **149**.19-20
    financial abuse **159**.16
    money management **180**.7-19
    students **180**.28-9, 32-3; **185**.2-3, 11
    worries and depression **190**.5
    see also banks; credit; debt; incomes; wages
monoamine oxidase inhibitors (MAOIs) **190**.11, 33
mood stabilising drugs **190**.10
moral decisions and humanism **148**.14-16
moral decline, Britain **148**.17
moral rights
    of animals **169**.1
    of embryos **178**.33-4
morphine **152**.26-7
mortality
    and depression **190**.20
    rates **150**.32
mortgages **181**.24, 28
    lifetime mortgages **180**.23
    mortgage lending **134**.25
Mosaic profiling system **149**.17
    education and social class **149**.32
Muslims *see* Islam
mosques
    improving governance standards **147**.34
    teaching in British mosques **147**.17-18
mothers
    and abortion rights **171**. 28
    abortion to save mother's life **171**.17, 22
    dieting, effect on daughters **184**.21-2
    effect on children's body image **170**.24; **184**.21-2
    employment patterns **149**.28; **154**.29
    HIV transmission to children **164**.3, 25, 27, 29-30, 31, 38
    identity confusion **149**.4-5

Volume numbers appear first (in bold) followed by page numbers; a change in volume number is preceded by a semi-**colon**.

Vol. 88 Food and Nutrition
Vol. 97 Energy Matters
Vol. 99 Exploited Children
Vol. 100 Stress and Anxiety
Vol. 119 Transport Trends
Vol. 129 Gambling Trends
Vol. 134 Customers and Consumerism
Vol. 138 A Genetically Modified Future?
Vol. 139 The Education Problem
Vol. 140 Vegetarian and Vegan Diets
Vol. 141 Mental Health
Vol. 142 Media Issues
Vol. 144 The Cloning Debate
Vol. 146 Sustainability and Environment
Vol. 147 The Terrorism Problem
Vol. 148 Religious Beliefs
Vol. 149 A Classless Society?
Vol. 150 Migration and Population
Vol. 151 Climate Change
Vol. 152 Euthanasia and the Right to Die
Vol. 153 Sexual Orientation and Society
Vol. 154 The Gender Gap
Vol. 155 Domestic Abuse

Vol. 156 Travel and Tourism
Vol. 157 The Problem of Globalisation
Vol. 158 The Internet Revolution
Vol. 159 An Ageing Population
Vol. 160 Poverty and Exclusion
Vol. 161 Waste Issues
Vol. 162 Staying Fit
Vol. 163 Drugs in the UK
Vol. 164 The AIDS Crisis
Vol. 165 Bullying Issues
Vol. 166 Marriage and Cohabitation
Vol. 167 Our Human Rights
Vol. 168 Privacy and Surveillance
Vol. 169 The Animal Rights Debate
Vol. 170 Body Image and Self-Esteem
Vol. 171 Abortion – Rights and Ethics
Vol. 172 Racial and Ethnic Discrimination
Vol. 173 Sexual Health
Vol. 174 Selling Sex
Vol. 175 Citizenship and Participation
Vol. 176 Health Issues for Young People
Vol. 177 Crime in the UK
Vol. 178 Reproductive Ethics

Vol. 179 Tackling Child Abuse
Vol. 180 Money and Finances
Vol. 181 The Housing Issue
Vol. 182 Teenage Conceptions
Vol. 183 Work and Employment
Vol. 184 Understanding Eating Disorders
Vol. 185 Student Matters
Vol. 186 Cannabis Use
Vol. 187 Health and the State
Vol. 188 Tobacco and Health
Vol. 189 The Homeless Population
Vol. 190 Coping with Depression
Vol. 191 The Changing Family
Vol. 192 Bereavement and Grief
Vol. 193 Endangered Species
Vol. 194 Responsible Drinking
Vol. 195 Alternative Medicine
Vol. 196 Censorship Issues
Vol. 197 Living with Disability
Vol. 198 Sport and Society
Vol. 199 Self-Harming and Suicide

maternity rights 191.37-8
and poverty 160.15
preferring not to work 183.25
stay-at-home mothers suffering stress 191.35
see also working mothers
motor neurone disease (MND) and stem cell research 144.32-3
motoring
costs 119.14
and disability 197.11
spending on 134.4, 25
trends 119.7-9
see also cars
mourning *see* grief
movies *see* films
MPs
and the drugs debate 186.34-5
and General Elections 131.18
MRSA 187.28, 29
MSSA 187.28
multiculturalism
Britain 156.11
British Muslims support for 115.34
as hindrance to British identity 131.10
London 115.23
multi-faith schools 148.32-3
multi-infarct dementia (vascular dementia) 141.6
multinational corporations (MNCs) 157.6, 11
and anti-globalisation campaigners 157.30-31
employment 157.13
multiple births and IVF 178.6-7
health problems 178.21-2
multiple embryo transfers 178.8
multiple identity concept of national identity 131.10
multiple personality disorder 141.12
multiple sclerosis (MS), classification as disability 197.1
multiracialism, Britain 115.3, 23, 24-5, 38
muscular dystrophies 197.3
Muslims
British, feelings of identity 131.9
fears after London bombings 115.36
protests against British soldiers 196.9-10
support for integration 115.34
young Muslims and fundamentalism 147.16-17
see also Islam

N

nalmefene 129.39
NAM (Non-Aligned Movement) 157.6-7
NAMA (non-agricultural market access) 157.14
name changing and civil partnerships 153.28
names for racial identity 115.4-5
nappies, waste disposal 161.1 5, 29
National Curriculum 139.1-2, 5-6
pupils opinions 139.7
and specialist diplomas 139.25
National DNA Database 168.7, 11-12
National Health Service *see* NHS
national identity 131.1-14

cards *see* identity cards
effect of devolution 131.6
and ethnic groups 131.8
non-white ethnic groups 115.38
National Identity Register 168.15, 17, 19
National Identity Scheme 168.14-19
National Institute for Clinical Excellence (NICE) *see* NICE
National Lottery 129.9-13
disability sports funding 198.18
good causes 129.9
Olympic Games funding 129.9
online, and under 16s 129.12-13
and social mobility 149.22
and under 16s 129.11-13
national origin as grounds for discrimination 115.7
nationalist-separatist terrorism 147.1
nationality as grounds for discrimination 115.7
natural burial 134.31
natural cloning 144.1
natural family planning 182.19
natural gas vehicles 119.20-21
natural medicine *see* complementary medicine (CM)
natural resources 146.9
nearest relative under Mental Health Act 190.11
NEETs (young people not in employment, education or training) 183.32
negative body image *see* body image, negative
negative resource transfers 157.7
negative thinking 170.6
neglect
children 179.3
reporting 179.7
signs 179.5
taking children into care 179.10-11
and older people 159.17
net neutrality 158.24
Netherlands, The
doctor-assisted suicide 152.31
euthanasia cases 152.7
euthanasia legislation 152.4, 11, 18, 19
extremist parties 131.23
sex education 182.28-9, 32-4
neurosis 141.1
neurotransmitters 141.9
news
attitudes to 142.31-3
being interviewed 142.11-12
effect of media ownership 142.5
sources 142.33
women in news media 154.11
newspapers 142.8-9
advertising 134.8
cartoons of Muhammed 142.34
and Freedom of Information Act 142.17
mergers 142.4
readership 142.8
sales 142.9
as source of news 142.33
NGOs *see* non-governmental organisations
NHS (National Health Service) 149.13-14; 187.1-23
achievements 187.25-6

anti-bullying strategies **165**.36
anti-smoking strategies, pregnant women **188**.30-32
constitution **187**.12-15
costs of smoking **188**.22
criticisms of **187**.26
  by US politicans **187**.19-20
disability discrimination **197**.30, 38-9
and eating disorders **184**.36
funding **187**.1, 3, 25, 26, 30
  patients' views **187**.11-12, 16-17
future proposals **187**.32-9
and herbal medicine **195**.11
and HIV treatments **96**.21, 22
and homeopathy **195**.16, 17-22, 24-5
  funding debate **195**.16, 17, 20-21
international comparisons **187**.4, 20-21
and older people **159**.4
patients' views **187**.11-12, 16-17
patients with learning difficulties **197**.38-9
performance **187**.1, 20-21
problems **187**.25-31
quality of care **187**.4, 26-8
reform strategy **187**.38-9
self-harm treatment **199**.13-14, 15, 18
size **187**.1, 3
statistics **187**.1, 3, 5-6
waiting times **187**.20-21
workforce **187**.2, 3
NICE (National Institute for Clinical Excellence) **187**.6, 21, 22-3
drink-driving study **194**.32
guidelines on eating disorders **184**.36
guidelines on reducing alcohol-related harm **194**.33, 36-8
nicotine
  addiction **188**.10, 16
  effects on heart **188**.7
  poisoning, tobacco pickers **188**.39
nicotine replacement therapies **188**.6
  VAT on **188**.23
night shelters *see* hostels for homeless people
nitrogen oxide (NOx) emissions **146**.35

agriculture **151**.7
  transport **119**.15, 16
non-agricultural market access (NAMA) **157**.14
non-contributory benefits **160**.23
non-governmental organisations (NGOs) **157**.7
non-means tested benefits **160**.23
non-native species, impact of **193**.12
  UK **193**.38-9
non-reproductive cloning *see* therapeutic cloning
non-traditional jobs for women **154**.31-2
non-voluntary euthanasia **152**.1, 3
Northern Ireland *see* Ireland, Northern
nuclear power **97**.3-4, 19-23; **151**.29
  building new power stations **97**.21-2
  and clean-up of nuclear weapons material **97**.23
  and climate change **97**.19-20, 21, 22
  costs of **97**.6
  debate over **97**.7
  disadvantages of **97**.2, 7, 8
  and electricity generation **97**.3-4, 22-3
  environmental issues surrounding **97**.2, 4
  and nuclear waste **97**.20, 22, 23
  and radioactive discharges **97**.20
  and renewable energy **97**.6, 7, 19, 21
  and terrorism **97**.20
nurses
  migration from developing countries **150**.15
  to have degree qualification **187**.33-5
nutrition
  and ageing **159**.2
  and meat **140**.12, 14
  and mental health **141**.30-31, 34
  and need for intensive farming **169**.12
  teenagers **176**.8-9
  vegetarians **140**.3-4, 6, 11
NVQs (National Vocational Qualifications) **139**.4

O

obesity **88**.4, 9-11; **162**.1-10
  and alcohol **194**.18

Volume numbers appear first (in bold) followed by page numbers; a change in volume number is preceded by a semi-**colon.**

Vol. 88 Food and Nutrition
Vol. 97 Energy Matters
Vol. 99 Exploited Children
Vol. 100 Stress and Anxiety
Vol. 119 Transport Trends
Vol. 129 Gambling Trends
Vol. 134 Customers and Consumerism
Vol. 138 A Genetically Modified Future?
Vol. 139 The Education Problem
Vol. 140 Vegetarian and Vegan Diets
Vol. 141 Mental Health
Vol. 142 Media Issues
Vol. 144 The Cloning Debate
Vol. 146 Sustainability and Environment
Vol. 147 The Terrorism Problem
Vol. 148 Religious Beliefs
Vol. 149 A Classless Society?
Vol. 150 Migration and Population
Vol. 151 Climate Change
Vol. 152 Euthanasia and the Right to Die
Vol. 153 Sexual Orientation and Society
Vol. 154 The Gender Gap
Vol. 155 Domestic Abuse

Vol. 156 Travel and Tourism
Vol. 157 The Problem of Globalisation
Vol. 158 The Internet Revolution
Vol. 159 An Ageing Population
Vol. 160 Poverty and Exclusion
Vol. 161 Waste Issues
Vol. 162 Staying Fit
Vol. 163 Drugs in the UK
Vol. 164 The AIDS Crisis
Vol. 165 Bullying Issues
Vol. 166 Marriage and Cohabitation
Vol. 167 Our Human Rights
Vol. 168 Privacy and Surveillance
Vol. 169 The Animal Rights Debate
Vol. 170 Body Image and Self-Esteem
Vol. 171 Abortion – Rights and Ethics
Vol. 172 Racial and Ethnic Discrimination
Vol. 173 Sexual Health
Vol. 174 Selling Sex
Vol. 175 Citizenship and Participation
Vol. 176 Health Issues for Young People
Vol. 177 Crime in the UK
Vol. 178 Reproductive Ethics

Vol. 179 Tackling Child Abuse
Vol. 180 Money and Finances
Vol. 181 The Housing Issue
Vol. 182 Teenage Conceptions
Vol. 183 Work and Employment
Vol. 184 Understanding Eating Disorders
Vol. 185 Student Matters
Vol. 186 Cannabis Use
Vol. 187 Health and the State
Vol. 188 Tobacco and Health
Vol. 189 The Homeless Population
Vol. 190 Coping with Depression
Vol. 191 The Changing Family
Vol. 192 Bereavement and Grief
Vol. 193 Endangered Species
Vol. 194 Responsible Drinking
Vol. 195 Alternative Medicine
Vol. 196 Censorship Issues
Vol. 197 Living with Disability
Vol. 198 Sport and Society
Vol. 199 Self-Harming and Suicide

avoidance *see* weight management
and Body Mass Index (BMI) **162**.1, 4, 5, 23
and bullying **165**.8-9
causes **162**.2, 5, 8
in children *see* childhood obesity
definitions **162**.1, 4
discrimination **162**.21
economic costs **88**.4
government strategies **162**.4-5, 9-10, 17-18, 22-3
    potential harm **184**.33
and health **162**.1-2, 5, 6, 7, 19, 25; **176**.7
and life expectancy **176**.7
measurement **162**.1
predictions **162**.10, 18, 19
statistics **162**.1, 5, 6, 7, 18; **187**.4
treatment **162**.2-3, 6, 20
in the workplace **162**.21
worldwide **162**.7
and young people **176**.2, 3, 7, 9
obscenity **196**.22-3
obsessions **141**.17
with food **184**.9-11
obsessive compulsive disorder (OCD) **141**.17
ocean acidification **193**.30
ocean plants and CO2 removal **151**.25
occupational choice, women **154**.30
non-traditional **154**.31-2
occupational social class **149**.21
occupational therapists **197**.4
Ofcom **196**.18-20
    and illegal broadcasting **142**.7
    and media mergers **142**.4
    and offensive language on television **196**.21, 24
offensive language
    and disabled people **197**.28-9
    television **196**.21, 24
offensive material
    broadcasters' rights **196**.24
    cartoons in airport prayer room **196**.11-12
official debt **157**.7
offsetting carbon **151**.20-22, 33-5
offshore wind farms **97**.12, 16, 26
offshoring **157**.35-6
oil
    depletion of resources **97**.8, 10
    leakages **97**.3
    recycling **161**.5, 23, 28
    and renewable energy **97**.10
older people
    abuse of **159**.4, 6, 16-18
    as carers **159**.4, 5
    and health **159**.4, 6, 8, 35-9
    in employment **159**.10, 15
    media consumption **158**.4
    and mental health problems **141**.2
    spending **159**.19
    and suicide **199**.20, 21
    worldwide **159**.5, 6
    UK **159**.3-4, 7-8
older women
    and eating disorders **184**.14-15

and IVF **178**.17, 19-20
older workers **159**.10, 15; **183**.15, 27
    and age discrimination **159**.4, 8-13
Olympic Games
    and China's human rights **167**.23-4
    gender equality **198**.19
    National Lottery funding **129**.9
    and sports competition for young people **198**.5
    talent identification **198**.8-10
    see also Paralympic Games
omega 3 fatty acids
    and attention-deficit hyperactivity disorder **141**.19
    in eggs **140**.39
    in meat **140**.12, 21
online brands **142**.35
online bullying *see* cyberbullying
online child sexual abuse **179**.15-16, 17
online communities and travel information **156**.14
online crime **158**.3, 33-4, 35, 36
online dating scams **134**.27
online divorces **166**.27
online entertainments **158**.21-2
online fraud **134**.26-9
online gambling **129**.17-18, 19-25
    and addiction **129**.21-2
    Europe **129**.20
    National Lottery games and under 16s **129**.12-13
    participation rates **129**.17, 19
    poker, underage **129**.25
    at work **129**.22-4
online gaming addiction **158**.39
online learning **139**.28
online retail *see* Internet shopping
online safety, social networking **179**.18
online surveillance **168**.13-14, 32-3
online terrorism **147**.8-9
online travel booking **156**.1, 13, 14; **158**.3
opiates/opioids **163**.5, 25
opium production **163**.25
Oregon State, euthanasia **152**.4, 18, 19, 31, 33
organ donation **192**.28
    and HIV transmission **164**.1
organ transplants *see* therapeutic cloning
organic farming **146**.25, 27
    animal welfare **140**.35-6
    meat production **140**.29-30
    unable to meet demand for food **140**.36-7
organic food **88**.13-14, 18, 33, 34
    and Fairtrade **134**.37
organic shops **134**.30, 31
organic waste, composting **161**.19, 28-9, 30
orphans, AIDS **96**.39; **164**.6-7
orthorexia nervosa **184**.9
osteoporosis and cannabis use **186**.6
out-of-school learning **139**.27-8
outdoor activities
    and interfaith relations **148**.31
outdoor (released) GMOs **138**.12
overdoses *see* drug overdoses
overdrafts **134**.22, 24; **180**.26-7
overseas students **139**.30, 31, 32

overseas travel trends **119**.1; **156**.1-2, 4-5

overseas visitors to UK **156**.3-4, 10, 13

overseas workers, UK dependence on **146**.6

overweight people

    children **119**.31

    see also obesity

ovulation disorders **178**.4

ownership of the media

    effect on news **142**.5

    mergers **142**.4

    newspapers **142**.9

Oxbridge

    entrance tests **185**.23

    school backgrounds of candidates **149**.34-5

    teachers' misconceptions about **185**.24

ozone and air pollution **146**.35

ozone layer depletion **151**.4

P

packaging waste **161**.4, 5, 12

paedophiles

    disclosure of **179**.20-21

    help for **179**.22-3

    see also child pornography; sex offenders

pain

    definition **152**.2

    rights of animals to avoid pain **169**.1

    suffered by experimental animals **169**.14-16

pain relief

    and cannabis **186**.16

    and placebo effect **195**.28-9

    see also palliative care

painkillers

    misuse **163**.14-15

    and sport **198**.28-9

Palestinian terrorist groups **147**.4

palliative care **152**.1-2, 5, 9, 22, 27

    effect of legalising euthanasia **152**.4

    limits of **152**.10

palm oil industry and biodiversity **193**.8-9

pancreas repair, stem cell therapy **144**.21

pancreatitis **194**.6

paper **161**.5, 22

    recycling **161**.24, 26

Paralympic Games **198**.20

    National Lottery funding **129**.9

    talent identification **198**.22

paranoia **141**.5

parental child abduction **166**.36

parental leave **183**.18, 22, 24, 27; **191**.34, 39

    for adoption **178**.16

parental relationships

    effect on children **166**.4-5, 29-32; **191**.1

    and youth homelessness **189**.27

parental responsibility **153**.33; **166**.26-7, 34

    cohabiting parents **166**.14-15

parental rights **153**.33-4

parental separation, effect on children **191**.1, 9

parenting orders **177**.18

parents

    and adult children **191**.26-8

    and alcohol

        alcohol abuse **194**.27-8

        influence on children's drinking **194**.25-6

    and child labour **99**.3

    and children as consumers **134**.12

    and children's body image **170**.24

    and children's mental health **176**.29-30

    cohabiting **166**.14-15

    and corporal punishment **179**.30, 33, 35

    death of a child **192**.20-23

    education as factor in university application **149**.7, 31

    empty nest syndrome disproved **191**.29

    of lesbians and gay people **153**.9-10

    with mental health problems **141**.24-5

    parenting styles **191**.5

        influence on children's character **191**.191.6

    removing children from **179**.10-11

    rights to information on sex offenders **179**.20-21

    same-sex **153**.20-22

    sex education role **182**.34-5

    and smacking **179**.33

Volume numbers appear first (in bold) followed by page numbers; a change in volume number is preceded by a semi-**colon.**

Vol. 88 Food and Nutrition

Vol. 97 Energy Matters

Vol. 99 Exploited Children

Vol. 100 Stress and Anxiety

Vol. 119 Transport Trends

Vol. 129 Gambling Trends

Vol. 134 Customers and Consumerism

Vol. 138 A Genetically Modified Future?

Vol. 139 The Education Problem

Vol. 140 Vegetarian and Vegan Diets

Vol. 141 Mental Health

Vol. 142 Media Issues

Vol. 144 The Cloning Debate

Vol. 146 Sustainability and Environment

Vol. 147 The Terrorism Problem

Vol. 148 Religious Beliefs

Vol. 149 A Classless Society?

Vol. 150 Migration and Population

Vol. 151 Climate Change

Vol. 152 Euthanasia and the Right to Die

Vol. 153 Sexual Orientation and Society

Vol. 154 The Gender Gap

Vol. 155 Domestic Abuse

Vol. 156 Travel and Tourism

Vol. 157 The Problem of Globalisation

Vol. 158 The Internet Revolution

Vol. 159 An Ageing Population

Vol. 160 Poverty and Exclusion

Vol. 161 Waste Issues

Vol. 162 Staying Fit

Vol. 163 Drugs in the UK

Vol. 164 The AIDS Crisis

Vol. 165 Bullying Issues

Vol. 166 Marriage and Cohabitation

Vol. 167 Our Human Rights

Vol. 168 Privacy and Surveillance

Vol. 169 The Animal Rights Debate

Vol. 170 Body Image and Self-Esteem

Vol. 171 Abortion – Rights and Ethics

Vol. 172 Racial and Ethnic Discrimination

Vol. 173 Sexual Health

Vol. 174 Selling Sex

Vol. 175 Citizenship and Participation

Vol. 176 Health Issues for Young People

Vol. 177 Crime in the UK

Vol. 178 Reproductive Ethics

Vol. 179 Tackling Child Abuse

Vol. 180 Money and Finances

Vol. 181 The Housing Issue

Vol. 182 Teenage Conceptions

Vol. 183 Work and Employment

Vol. 184 Understanding Eating Disorders

Vol. 185 Student Matters

Vol. 186 Cannabis Use

Vol. 187 Health and the State

Vol. 188 Tobacco and Health

Vol. 189 The Homeless Population

Vol. 190 Coping with Depression

Vol. 191 The Changing Family

Vol. 192 Bereavement and Grief

Vol. 193 Endangered Species

Vol. 194 Responsible Drinking

Vol. 195 Alternative Medicine

Vol. 196 Censorship Issues

Vol. 197 Living with Disability

Vol. 198 Sport and Society

Vol. 199 Self-Harming and Suicide

smoking, influence on young people smoking **188**.28
and stress **100**.13
stay-at-home parents **191**.35
and student finance **139**.34, 35
support for first-time buyers **181**.1
supporting adult children **191**.26-8
and teenage depression **190**.27
young parents **182**.14-18
parking, illegal **119**.9
Parkinson's disease and dementia **141**.6
Parliament **131**.15
parliamentary authority and Human Rights Act **167**.5
women in **154**.4, 6, 12
part-time jobs
and the pay gap **154**.6, 36
and students **139**.35
partial (host) surrogacy **178**.7, 13
particulates emissions **119**.15
passive euthanasia **152**.5
passive smoking **188**.5, 10-11, 12
patents **138**.4
genes **138**.23
paternity leave **183**.18, 22, 24; **191**.34-5, 39
pathological gambling *see* compulsive gambling
patients
GP survey **187**.16-17
relationship with GPs **187**.31
rights **187**.13-15, 32-3
and doctors' rights, abortion **171**.28
to refuse treatment **152**.2, 10-11
standards of care **187**.4, 26-8
patriotic hacking **196**.34-5
pay gap *see* gender pay gap
PBRM1 gene and depression **190**.12-13
pedestrians and road accidents **119**.5, 30-31
peer education programmes, HIV/AIDS **164**.18
peer mentoring
anti-bullying **165**.18
young parents **182**.39
peer pressure and drinking behaviour **194**.12
peer support
and bullying **165**.18
and suicide **199**.33
peer-to-peer (P2P) downloading **158**.36
penalties
cannabis supply **186**.2, 30
for drug smuggling **163**.38
possession of cannabis **186**.1-2, 5, 9, 30
penalty notices **177**.8, 25
pensions
and civil partnerships **153**.28
claiming after a death **192**.32-3
Europe **159**.25
gender gap **154**.6
saving for **134**.4, 25; **159**.21, 22; **180**.8
graduates **139**.36
UK **159**.3, 23, 25
universal social pension **159**.24
permissive behaviour and the media **196**.25-6
personal crime, racial identity of victims **115**.10
personal information **168**.31

concerns about **168**.37
control of **158**.31-4
and Data Protection Act **168**.10-11
protecting **168**.31-2, 37
personal privacy **168**.31-9
personal skills gap **149**.37-8
personalisation of care **197**.13
pesco-vegetarian diet **140**.2
pester power **134**.12
pesticides **88**.13, 32, 34, 35
GM viruses **138**.13-14
petrol prices **119**.12-13, 14
see also fuel taxes
pets, exotic
demand for, impact on biodiversity in Asia **193**.20-21
impact on British wildlife **193**.39
pharmaceutical industry **163**.1
pharming **138**.4, 9-10, 20-22
hens for cancer treatment **138**.20-21
rice **138**.20
risks **138**.20, 21, 22
tobacco plants for HIV treatment **138**.21-2
phishing **134**.27-8, 28-9; **158**.33-4
phobias **141**.16-17
and young people **100**.2
physical abuse
bullying
children with learning diabilities **165**.15
disabled people **165**.17
of children **179**.1-2, 5
of older people **159**.16
signs of **179**.5
and stress **100**.1, 2
physical activity *see* exercise
physical disabilities **197**.3-5
physical punishment *see* corporal punishment
physician-assisted suicide (PAS) **152**.4, 7-8, 29-30, 31
see also assisted suicide
physiotherapists **197**.4
phytochemicals **88**.5, 7, 13
phytoplankton **193**.5
pill, contraceptive **176**.27; **182**.19
over the counter availability **182**.21-3
pink plateau **153**.39
placebo effect **195**.28-9
and complementary medicine **195**.26, 27
plagiarism and the Internet **158**.2, 19-20
plants
and photosynthesis **97**.9
see also genetically modified (GM) crops
plasmids **138**.2
plastic bags **161**.5, 13-14, 19, 36-7
plastic surgery *see* cosmetic surgery
plastic waste **161**.5, 22, 29
recycling **161**.24, 29
play and disabled children **197**.37
poisoning, emergency treatment **199**.14
poker, online, and underage gambling **129**.25
police **177**.33-4
arrest, your rights **177**.35-6
concerns about migrant crime **150**.12

domestic violence units **155**.29

drug classification, effects on policing **186**.36-7

and drugs offences **163**.38

and online child pornography **99**.24

stop and search **177**.34

and Terrorism Act **147**.3

stop and search powers **147**.35-7

young people's attitudes to **177**.15-16

political broadcasting, Ofcom regulation **196**.19

political media, women in **154**.11

political and military globalisation **157**.2

political overreaction to terrorism **147**.10-11, 38-9

political parties **131**.18

BNP inclusion in political debates **196**.7, 8

housing policies **181**.23

views on hunting **169**.28

young peoples's support **131**.32

politics

and genomics **138**.3

and gender equality **154**.4, 6, 12, 21

and human rights **167**.4-5

and the hunting debate **169**.27-9

and the media **142**.2

and newspapers **142**.8

older people's engagement in **159**.7

recommendations for change **131**.25

young people's involvement **131**.27-35

see also elections

pollinating insects, decliing numbers **193**.27-8

pollution

from aviation **119**.16

effects on wildlife **193**.2

and transport **119**.12, 13-14, 16, 30, 31; **146**.35-6

see also emissions, transport

see also air pollution; water pollution

population **150**.28-39

ageing population **159**.3, 6

and development goals **150**.34

global trends **150**.34-5; **159**.6

information from census **150**.36

and poverty **150**.34

sustainable **150**.31-2

population changes

see ageing population; population growth

population control to combat climate change **151**.31-2

population growth

and the environment **146**.12-13, 16-17; **150**.27

global **150**.31, 32-3, 34

and immigration **150**.16

UK **150**.28, 29, 31

pornography

and the Internet **158**.3

children viewing **196**.38

see also child pornography

port policing strategy, anti-terrorism **147**.29

positive action and age discrimination **159**.9-10

positive body image **170**.17, 37

positive discrimination **154**.36

positive thinking **141**.36

possession of cannabis **186**.1-2, 5, 9, 30

post-compulsory education **139**.2

see also A-levels; higher education; universities

post-mortem, hospital **192**.31

post-natal depression **190**.2, 14-17, 21-2

fathers **190**.16-17

mothers **190**.16-17

and suicide risk **190**.24

symptoms of **190**.14

post-traumatic stress disorder (PTSD) **141**.3, 12; **176**.30

postal voting **131**.16

postcodes and population profiling **149**.17

postgraduate destinations **185**.32

postgraduate study **185**.30

potatoes, GM research trials **138**.27, 28

poverty

attitudes to **160**.3, 4

causes of **160**.2, 25-6

and child labour **99**.2, 3, 4, 14-15

children living in *see* child poverty

children's perceptions of **149**.9-12; **160**.4

and children's wellbeing **191**.9

and debt **160**.12, 33

definitions **160**.1, 25, 26

and disabled people **160**.10; **197**.35

Volume numbers appear first (in bold) followed by page numbers; a change in volume number is preceded by a semi-**colon**.

Vol. 88 Food and Nutrition
Vol. 97 Energy Matters
Vol. 99 Exploited Children
Vol. 100 Stress and Anxiety
Vol. 119 Transport Trends
Vol. 129 Gambling Trends
Vol. 134 Customers and Consumerism
Vol. 138 A Genetically Modified Future?
Vol. 139 The Education Problem
Vol. 140 Vegetarian and Vegan Diets
Vol. 141 Mental Health
Vol. 142 Media Issues
Vol. 144 The Cloning Debate
Vol. 146 Sustainability and Environment
Vol. 147 The Terrorism Problem
Vol. 148 Religious Beliefs
Vol. 149 A Classless Society?
Vol. 150 Migration and Population
Vol. 151 Climate Change
Vol. 152 Euthanasia and the Right to Die
Vol. 153 Sexual Orientation and Society
Vol. 154 The Gender Gap
Vol. 155 Domestic Abuse

Vol. 156 Travel and Tourism
Vol. 157 The Problem of Globalisation
Vol. 158 The Internet Revolution
Vol. 159 An Ageing Population
Vol. 160 Poverty and Exclusion
Vol. 161 Waste Issues
Vol. 162 Staying Fit
Vol. 163 Drugs in the UK
Vol. 164 The AIDS Crisis
Vol. 165 Bullying Issues
Vol. 166 Marriage and Cohabitation
Vol. 167 Our Human Rights
Vol. 168 Privacy and Surveillance
Vol. 169 The Animal Rights Debate
Vol. 170 Body Image and Self-Esteem
Vol. 171 Abortion – Rights and Ethics
Vol. 172 Racial and Ethnic Discrimination
Vol. 173 Sexual Health
Vol. 174 Selling Sex
Vol. 175 Citizenship and Participation
Vol. 176 Health Issues for Young People
Vol. 177 Crime in the UK
Vol. 178 Reproductive Ethics

Vol. 179 Tackling Child Abuse
Vol. 180 Money and Finances
Vol. 181 The Housing Issue
Vol. 182 Teenage Conceptions
Vol. 183 Work and Employment
Vol. 184 Understanding Eating Disorders
Vol. 185 Student Matters
Vol. 186 Cannabis Use
Vol. 187 Health and the State
Vol. 188 Tobacco and Health
Vol. 189 The Homeless Population
Vol. 190 Coping with Depression
Vol. 191 The Changing Family
Vol. 192 Bereavement and Grief
Vol. 193 Endangered Species
Vol. 194 Responsible Drinking
Vol. 195 Alternative Medicine
Vol. 196 Censorship Issues
Vol. 197 Living with Disability
Vol. 198 Sport and Society
Vol. 199 Self-Harming and Suicide

and education **160**.16-22
and environmental stress **146**.16-17
experiences of **160**.13-14, 27
extent of **160**.1-2
and free trade **157**.9, 13, 26-7
global **160**.25-39
and global financial crisis **180**.1
government action **160**.21-2
and government debt **157**.9-10
and health **149**.14; **160**.2
and HIV/AIDS **96**.24, 29; **164**.10, 27
impact of **160**.2, 13-14
lone parent families **191**.1
measuring **160**.1, 8
and mental health problems **141**.2, 22
and Millennium Development Goals **160**.30
and older people **159**.3
and population **150**.34
and post traumatic stress disorder **141**.3
rich-poor gap
   global **160**.26, 29
   UK **115**.32; **149**.19, 20, 22, 27, 29; **160**.6, 7
and segregation **115**.30, 31, 32
and the sexual exploitation of children **99**.16, 24
statistics **160**.1-2, 25, 29
in the UK **160**.1-24
and urbanisation **150**.38
and women **160**.15
poverty line **160**.1
power gap **154**.4, 6
powers of dispersal **177**.8
prayer **148**.1
pre-implantation genetic diagnosis **144**.20; **178**.2, 28-9,
   30-31, 31-2
pre-marital sex, attitudes to **166**.1
pre-paid cards **180**.26
pre-school children
   gender differences **154**.24
   effects of poverty **160**.20
precursor cells **144**.25
pregnancy **178**.2-3; **182**.3-5
   and alcohol **194**.14
   and domestic violence **155**.11, 30
   employment rights **191**.37-8
   and exercise **162**.32
   and HIV **96**.16, 22, 23, 31, 38; **164**.3, 25, 27, 29-30, 31
   risks **182**.11, 37
   and school **182**.6
   and smoking **88**.7; **188**.11, 31
     NHS anti-smoking strategies **188**.30-32
   testing **182**.4-5
   your choices **182**.6, 8-9
   see also abortion; teenage pregnancies
prejudice
   against bisexuals **153**.10
   and bullying **165**.8-9
   definition **115**.4
   fears of parents of gay children **153**.9
   Islamaphobia **115**.36
   racial **131**.2
   religious **131**.3

and sexual orientation **153**.2
   against transgender people **153**.13
   see also discrimination; homophobia
premature babies
   treatment decisions **152**.4, 32, 34
   viability **171**.23-4, 29, 31
prenatal screening **171**.22
prescription drugs, misuse **163**.14-16
Press Code **142**.26
Press Complaints Commission **142**.26, 30; **196**.3
   and Jan Moir article on Stephen Gately **196**.3, 4-5
   and suicide reporting **142**.30
press conferences **142**.12-13
press freedom **196**.1-2
press intrusion **168**.28-9
press regulation, public opinion **196**.6
price of alcohol **194**.35
   minimum pricing **194**.36, 37
Primary Care Trusts (PCTs) **187**.5
primary schools
   curriculum **139**.5, 6
   and gay issues **153**.19-20
   gender gap **154**.23
   and homophobic bullying **153**.15
   and pupils' mental health **141**.37
   see also schools
primates
   endangered species **193**.22-3
   use in research **169**.24-6
   with jellyfish genes **144**.11
prison **177**.39
   prison leavers and homelessness **189**.6
   prison sentences **177**.25, 37
     for knife crime **177**.38
   suicide rate **199**.25
   women prisoners and self-harm **199**.12
   see also youth custody
privacy **168**.1-3, 28-30
   definition **168**.1
   and the media **142**.25, 26; 7, 28-9
   and National Identity Scheme **168**.15
   protection, models of **168**.2
   rights **168**.1, 2-3; **196**.38
   and social networking **168**.35-6
   see also freedom of information
privacy-invading software and domestic abuse **155**.15-16
private healthcare **187**.24
private sales and consumer rights **134**.20
private schoolchildren
   attitudes to social differences **149**.9-12
   children's perceptions of **149**.11-12
private schools
   and children with learning problems **197**.15
   and university entrance **149**.34-5
pro-choice arguments **171**.32-3
   presentations to schools **171**.38
pro-eating disorder websites **184**.25-7
pro-life arguments **171**.21-3, 31
pro-life movement
   presentations to schools **171**.38
problem debt **134**.23

problem drinking *see* alcohol abuse
problem gambling *see* compulsive gambling
production, sustainable **146**.7, 8
professions and social mobility **185**.38-9
prohibited steps order **166**.27, 35
propaganda, terrorist, online **147**.8
property rights
    and cohabitation **166**.14
    disabled people **197**.21-2
prostitution, children **167**.32
protectionism **157**.7, 13, 23-4
proteins **88**.6, 8
    definition **138**.4
    drugs produced by GM hens **138**.20-21
    teenage requirements **176**.8
    and vegan diet **140**.23-4
    and vegetarian diet **140**.3, 7
psychedelic drugs **163**.2, 6
psychological abuse of older people **159**.16
psychological effects
    of abortion **171**.9-10
    of cannabis **186**.7-8, 9-13, 16, 28-9, 30, 31, 32
psychologists, and young people and stress **100**.2
psychology
    of class **149**.6
    and gambling **129**.6, 29
    and religion **148**.12-13
psychosis **141**.1
    and cannabis use **186**.10, 12, 13, 31, 32
psychotherapy
    and bipolar disorder **141**.14-15
    and depression **190**.5, 11, 34
    and eating disorders **184**.37
    lack of availability **190**.37
    and young people and stress **100**.2
psychotic depression **190**.2
PTSD (post-traumatic stress disorder) **141**.3, 12; **176**.30
public attitudes
    to abortion **171**.8, 16, 30, 34
    to anti-terror measures **167**.24
    to biotechnology **138**.15-16; **144**.19
    to bullfighting **169**.38

    to crime **177**.6, 23
    to euthanasia **152**.8, 12, 13, 15, 17
    to film classification **196**.15-16
    to the fur trade **169**.6
    to genetic modification **138**.3; **144**.20
    to human cloning **144**.35
    to human rights **167**.19
    to hunting with dogs **169**.29, 36
    to ID cards **168**.16
    to legal protection for gay people **153**.36
    to marriage and cohabitation **166**.1-2
    to mental ill-health **141**.25, 27
    to migrants **150**.3, 13-14, 17, 18-19
    to poverty **160**.3
    to press self-regulation **196**.6
    to smacking **179**.32
    terrorism fears **147**.12
public figures and privacy **168**.36
public grief **192**.7-8
    memorial websites **192**.38-9
public interest
    and journalists' rights **142**.27
    and media mergers **142**.4
public service broadcasting, news coverage **142**.33
public services
    and gender equality **154**.3
    and National Identity Scheme **168**.16
public transport **119**.1, 12, 25
    and disabled people **197**.11-12, 23
    encouraging use of **119**.39
    passes and personal data monitoring **168**.9
    usage **151**.39
puerperal psychosis **190**.15
punishment
    in schools, and racism **115**.19
pyramid selling **134**.26

Q

qualifications **139**.4
    and ethnicity **139**.8

Volume numbers appear first (in bold) followed by page numbers; a change in volume number is preceded by a semi-**colon**.

Vol. 88 Food and Nutrition
Vol. 97 Energy Matters
Vol. 99 Exploited Children
Vol. 100 Stress and Anxiety
Vol. 119 Transport Trends
Vol. 129 Gambling Trends
Vol. 134 Customers and Consumerism
Vol. 138 A Genetically Modified Future?
Vol. 139 The Education Problem
Vol. 140 Vegetarian and Vegan Diets
Vol. 141 Mental Health
Vol. 142 Media Issues
Vol. 144 The Cloning Debate
Vol. 146 Sustainability and Environment
Vol. 147 The Terrorism Problem
Vol. 148 Religious Beliefs
Vol. 149 A Classless Society?
Vol. 150 Migration and Population
Vol. 151 Climate Change
Vol. 152 Euthanasia and the Right to Die
Vol. 153 Sexual Orientation and Society
Vol. 154 The Gender Gap
Vol. 155 Domestic Abuse

Vol. 156 Travel and Tourism
Vol. 157 The Problem of Globalisation
Vol. 158 The Internet Revolution
Vol. 159 An Ageing Population
Vol. 160 Poverty and Exclusion
Vol. 161 Waste Issues
Vol. 162 Staying Fit
Vol. 163 Drugs in the UK
Vol. 164 The AIDS Crisis
Vol. 165 Bullying Issues
Vol. 166 Marriage and Cohabitation
Vol. 167 Our Human Rights
Vol. 168 Privacy and Surveillance
Vol. 169 The Animal Rights Debate
Vol. 170 Body Image and Self-Esteem
Vol. 171 Abortion – Rights and Ethics
Vol. 172 Racial and Ethnic Discrimination
Vol. 173 Sexual Health
Vol. 174 Selling Sex
Vol. 175 Citizenship and Participation
Vol. 176 Health Issues for Young People
Vol. 177 Crime in the UK
Vol. 178 Reproductive Ethics

Vol. 179 Tackling Child Abuse
Vol. 180 Money and Finances
Vol. 181 The Housing Issue
Vol. 182 Teenage Conceptions
Vol. 183 Work and Employment
Vol. 184 Understanding Eating Disorders
Vol. 185 Student Matters
Vol. 186 Cannabis Use
Vol. 187 Health and the State
Vol. 188 Tobacco and Health
Vol. 189 The Homeless Population
Vol. 190 Coping with Depression
Vol. 191 The Changing Family
Vol. 192 Bereavement and Grief
Vol. 193 Endangered Species
Vol. 194 Responsible Drinking
Vol. 195 Alternative Medicine
Vol. 196 Censorship Issues
Vol. 197 Living with Disability
Vol. 198 Sport and Society
Vol. 199 Self-Harming and Suicide

and gender **139**.10
  nurses **187**.33-5
  for university entrance **139**.29-30
  see also A-levels; AS-levels; degrees; educational
    achievement; GCSEs
qualified human rights **167**.4
quality of goods, consumer rights **134**.2, 17
questioning by police **177**.35
quitting smoking *see* smoking, giving up
Quorn **140**.19
quotas for migrant workers **150**.7
quotations and consumer rights **134**.18

R

rabbit-human embryos **144**.11
race
  and domestic violence **155**.4
  definition **115**.4
  as grounds for discrimination **115**.7
  names for **115**.4-5
race relations **147**.19
Race Relations Act **115**.2, 7-8
racial background, UK population **115**.3, 24-5
racial discrimination **115**.4, 7-8
  in employment **115**.13
  see also racism
racial harassment, defining **115**.8
racial identity
  confusion over **149**.4
  victims of crime **115**.10
racial integration **115**.6, 28-9; **131**.9; **147**.19
  Asians **115**.37
  in education **115**.29, 33
racial profiling and 'stop and search' **147**.35-6
Racial and Religious Hatred Bill **148**.29
racial segregation **115**.28-32
racially motivated crime **115**.9-10
racism **115**.1-2, 4
  challenging **115**.2
  and ChildLine **115**.1
  and children **115**.9
  defining **115**.4
  and education **115**.19-20
  effects of **115**.1
  and Islamophobia **115**.36
  laws **115**.2, 7-8, 11-12, 26
  perception of **131**.2
  reasons for **115**.1-2
  in schools **115**.9, 19-20; **139**.9
  in the workplace **115**.11-14
  see also discrimination; employment and racism; ethnic
    minorities; racial discrimination
racist bullying **115**.2; **165**.9
racist incidents **115**.9
radiation exposure due to smoking **188**.9
radio **158**.5, 6
  interviews **142**.13-14
  as news source **142**.33
  pirate stations **142**.7

railways
  congestion **119**.35
  and disabled people **197**.11
  travel trends **119**.1; **161**.31-2
rainforests *see* forests
rape
  as reason for abortion **171**.21-2
  as torture **167**.25-6
rate of return on education **139**.1, 37
reality TV, breaking ethnic stereotypes **115**.22
reasonable adjustments for disabled people
  education providers **197**.23
  service providers **197**.21
  workplace **197**.24
recession **180**.1-5
  definition **180**.2
  effects on employment **183**.1-2
  global **180**.1-2
  indicators **180**.5
  and lone parent families **191**.13
reclassification of cannabis **163**.32, 35-6; **186**.4-5, 32-3
  public opinion **186**.31
recombinant DNA technologies *see* genetic modification
recovered memory of sexual abuse **179**.26-9
recreational drugs use **163**.1
recruitment of employees
  Disability Symbol **197**.26-7
  discrimination **115**.13
  effects of recession **183**.1
recycling **161**.2, 18, 19, 22-9
  employment in **161**.2
  increase in **161**.31
  mobile phones **158**.13
  negative effects **161**.35
  organic waste *see* composting waste
  organizations **161**.9
  in public places **161**.20, 21
  reducing emissions **161**.3
  statistics **161**.22
  targets **161**.20
red squirrels, Scotland **193**.37
redress (compensation) **134**.2, 17
reduce, reuse, recycle **161**.7, 18
reducing waste **161**.18
  incentives for **161**.38
redundancy
  and disability discrimination **197**.24-5
  emotional impact **183**.10-11
  effect of recession **183**.2
referral orders **177**.17, 31
Refuge **155**.29, 32-3
refugees *see* asylum seekers
refuges **155**.12-13, 27-8, 32-3
regional differences, social class **149**.18
register of domestic violence offenders **155**.39
register of GM land **138**.19, 36
registering a death **192**.29-30
regulation
  animal experiments **169**.14, 20, 22
  broadcasters **196**.18-21
  of cloning **144**.3

of complementary therapists **195**.1, 3
of genetic modification **138**.3, 11
films **196**.13-16
of herbal medicines **195**.33, 34-5, 36, 37-8
of hybrid embryo research **144**.14
Internet **196**.31, 36-7
media
and civil liberties **142**.1-2
mergers **142**.4
online journalism **142**.16
obscene publications **196**.22-3
press **196**.6
stem cell cloning **144**.27-8
Regulation of Investigative Powers Act (RIPA) **168**.20, 21
relational elements of marriage **166**.2-3
relationships
dissolution **166**.3
see also divorce
and football supporting **141**.33
and human cloning **144**.6
and mental health **141**.34
mixed-faith **115**.39
mixed-race **115**.22-5
and mobile phones **158**.13
problems **166**.7-8
and suicide **199**.24
teaching about relationships **170**.14
teenage, and violence **179**.19
trends **191**.3-4
see also marriage
relaxation and stress **100**.29-30, 31-2, 34, 36-7
released (outdoor) GMOs **138**.12
religion **148**.1-39
and abortion **171**.17-19
and abortion education **171**.39
attitudes to **148**.26, 27
and attitudes to animals **169**.2
and the Census (2001) **148**.6-7
and corporal punishment **179**.36
and euthanasia **152**.7, 11, 12, 15, 34
and food rules **148**.10-11
functions **148**.1

funeral traditions **192**.34-6
and the law **148**.29
and moral decline **148**.17
religious observance in Britain **148**.6-8, 18-19, 25, 27
religious tolerance **148**.23-39
surveys **148**.8, 27
and terrorism **147**.1
theories of **148**.12-13
women in the workforce **154**.29
see also individual religions
religious discrimination **115**.26; **148**.28, 29
religious groups, segregation **115**.32
religious identity **115**.5, 26
religious marriage ceremonies **166**.6
religious offence **196**.11-12
religious prejudice, perception of **131**.3
religiously motivated crime **115**.27; **148**.29
terrorism **147**.1, 5
religious texts **148**.1
religious values **148**.16
remembrance of the deceased **192**.10
memorial websites **192**.38-9
see also funerals
remittances from migrants **150**.2
remote gambling **129**.17-26
remote sensing **168**.26-7
renewable energy **97**.6-18, 26; **151**.29-30
advantages of **97**.9
attitudes to **97**.5
bioenergy **97**.5, 6, 9, 11, 18
case for **97**.1-2, 6-7
costs of **97**.19, 38
defining **97**.8-9
electricity from **97**.4, 11, 37-8
future of **97**.8-9
hydroelectric power **97**.4, 5, 6, 12, 14, 38
and nuclear power **97**.6, 7, 19, 21
sources of **97**.4
types of **97**.9
in the UK **97**.13-14, 26, 39
see also energy efficiency; solar energy; wind energy
Renewables Obligation **151**.30

Volume numbers appear first (in bold) followed by page numbers; a change in volume number is preceded by a semi-colon.

Vol. 88 Food and Nutrition
Vol. 97 Energy Matters
Vol. 99 Exploited Children
Vol. 100 Stress and Anxiety
Vol. 119 Transport Trends
Vol. 129 Gambling Trends
Vol. 134 Customers and Consumerism
Vol. 138 A Genetically Modified Future?
Vol. 139 The Education Problem
Vol. 140 Vegetarian and Vegan Diets
Vol. 141 Mental Health
Vol. 142 Media Issues
Vol. 144 The Cloning Debate
Vol. 146 Sustainability and Environment
Vol. 147 The Terrorism Problem
Vol. 148 Religious Beliefs
Vol. 149 A Classless Society?
Vol. 150 Migration and Population
Vol. 151 Climate Change
Vol. 152 Euthanasia and the Right to Die
Vol. 153 Sexual Orientation and Society
Vol. 154 The Gender Gap
Vol. 155 Domestic Abuse

Vol. 156 Travel and Tourism
Vol. 157 The Problem of Globalisation
Vol. 158 The Internet Revolution
Vol. 159 An Ageing Population
Vol. 160 Poverty and Exclusion
Vol. 161 Waste Issues
Vol. 162 Staying Fit
Vol. 163 Drugs in the UK
Vol. 164 The AIDS Crisis
Vol. 165 Bullying Issues
Vol. 166 Marriage and Cohabitation
Vol. 167 Our Human Rights
Vol. 168 Privacy and Surveillance
Vol. 169 The Animal Rights Debate
Vol. 170 Body Image and Self-Esteem
Vol. 171 Abortion – Rights and Ethics
Vol. 172 Racial and Ethnic Discrimination
Vol. 173 Sexual Health
Vol. 174 Selling Sex
Vol. 175 Citizenship and Participation
Vol. 176 Health Issues for Young People
Vol. 177 Crime in the UK
Vol. 178 Reproductive Ethics

Vol. 179 Tackling Child Abuse
Vol. 180 Money and Finances
Vol. 181 The Housing Issue
Vol. 182 Teenage Conceptions
Vol. 183 Work and Employment
Vol. 184 Understanding Eating Disorders
Vol. 185 Student Matters
Vol. 186 Cannabis Use
Vol. 187 Health and the State
Vol. 188 Tobacco and Health
Vol. 189 The Homeless Population
Vol. 190 Coping with Depression
Vol. 191 The Changing Family
Vol. 192 Bereavement and Grief
Vol. 193 Endangered Species
Vol. 194 Responsible Drinking
Vol. 195 Alternative Medicine
Vol. 196 Censorship Issues
Vol. 197 Living with Disability
Vol. 198 Sport and Society
Vol. 199 Self-Harming and Suicide

rented accommodation
    as alternative to selling **181**.17
    disability rights **197**.21-2
    young people **181**.26, 33
reparation orders **177**.17, 31
repayment mortgages **181**.28
repossessed homes websites **181**.7
reproductive cloning **144**.15; **178**.36, 37
    see also human reproductive cloning
reprogrammed cells **144**.26
residence of children after divorce **166**.35
residential mobility **149**.26
resin, cannabis (hashish) **186**.2, 7, 9
resources
    natural **146**.9
    resource efficiency **146**.7
respiratory health
    and cannabis **186**.15, 28
    lung cancer **186**.15; **188**.6, 8
    and passive smoking **188**.5, 10-11
    and smoking **188**.5
responsible travel **134**.30; **156**.1, 20-39
    definition **156**.24
    see also ecotourism
restaurants
    and vegans **140**.25
    and vegetarians **140**.5
restorative justice **177**.31
retail industry
    and environmentalism **146**.38
    packaging waste **161**.12
    plastic bags **161**.13-14
retail therapy **134**.13
retirement
    feelings about **159**.15
    forced retirement **183**.14-15
    retiring abroad **150**.24
    saving for **159**.21, 22; **180**.8
    spending patterns, retired people **159**.19
    working after retirement age **159**.10, 15
    see also pensions
reusing goods **161**.18
Reverse Seasonal Affective Disorder **190**.7
Reynolds privilege **142**.27
rhinoceros, declining numbers **193**.1-2
rice, GM contamination **138**.20, 31-4
Rich Ordinary Britons (ROBs) **149**.19
rich-poor gap
    global **160**.26, 29
    UK **115**.32; **149**.19, 20, 22, 27, 29; **160**.6, 7
'right to buy' scheme, social housing **181**.25
right to move, council tenants **181**.35-6
right-wing terrorism **147**.1
righteous eating fixation **184**.9
rights
    in abortion
        of doctors **171**.27-28
        of the fetus **171**.17
        of women **171**.17, 20
    on arrest **177**.35-6
    children's *see* children's rights

consumer *see* consumer rights
    of migrant workers **150**.2
    to privacy **168**.2-3; **196**.38
    sexual **196**.36, 38
    young people **167**.28-39
    see also human rights
Rights of the Child, UN Convention on the **167**.28-9
Rio de Janeiro, shanty town tours **156**.34-5
road accidents **119**.4, 5, 28, 30-31
    and children **119**.5, 28, 30-31
    deaths **119**.4, 5, 28, 30
    and speed **119**.5, 30-31
    see also drink-driving
road building to ease congestion **119**.12
road charging **119**.35, 36
    congestion charging **119**.12, 34-5, 38
road safety **119**.4
    education **119**.5-6
    quiz **119**.6
road traffic **119**.1
    carbon offsetting **151**.22
    increase **119**.11, 13, 29
    injuries, children **119**.5, 28, 30-31
    pollution *see* pollution and transport
    see also cars
Robespierre, Maximilien **147**.4
roll-your-own cigarettes **188**.19
Roman Catholics *see* Catholic Church
Romanian migrants in UK **150**.6-7
Rotterdam, tours of deprived areas **156**.35
rough sleeping **189**.4, 16-17
    government targets **189**.8
    and mental health **189**.11
    young people **189**.23
    see also homelessness
round-the-world tickets **156**.15
Royal Mail, anti-bullying strategies **165**.36
RSPCA Freedom Food mark **140**.29, 34
rubbish *see* waste
runaways **189**.24, 25
running, effect on joints **162**.33
rural districts *see* countryside
Rwanda, human rights abuses **167**.13

S

sacred places **148**.1
SAD (Seasonal Affective Disorder) **141**.35; **190**.2, 6-7, 22
safe houses *see* refuges
safe sex **176**.22, 27, 28
safety
    of abortion **171**.3, 4, 11-12
    of complementary and alternative medicine **195**.2, 12-13, 34, 38
    and cycling **119**.28
    and gender equality **154**.3-4, 6
    of genetically modified crops **138**.6-6, 24
    of goods, consumer rights **134**.20
    and mobile phones **158**.13
    and self-harm **199**.6, 7-8

transport **119**.1

and walking to school **119**.26

at work, young people **183**.28

see also road safety

safety and the Internet **165**.26-7, 30-31

children and young people **158**.27-30

online shopping **158**.31

social networking **158**.9, 10-11; **179**.18

Sainsbury's

and fairtrade **157**.32

and plastic bags **161**.13

salaries

graduates **139**.35, 36, 37; **183**.36; **185**.32-4

teachers **139**.12

young people's expectations **180**.21-2

see also earnings; wages

salmonella **88**.28

salt intake **88**.2, 7, 10, 16, 23, 26

Samaritans **176**.35; **199**.20, 22, 31, 35

same-sex relationships

and domestic abuse **155**.13-15

having a child **178**.9-10

sanitation in developing countries **146**.14-15

Sarah's Law, dangers of **179**.20-21

Satanists and the census **148**.7

satellite surveillance **168**.26-7

saturated fats **88**.2, 22-3

savings

for old age **159**.21, 22; **180**.8

levels of **134**.25; **180**.7

savings accounts **180**.26

savings ratio **180**.7

and social class **149**.20

saviour siblings **178**.28-31

scabies **96**.7

scams **134**.26-9

Schengen Information System **168**.9

schizo affective disorder **190**.9

schizophrenia **141**.4-5; **185**.8

and cannabis use **186**.10, 12, 31, 32

school leavers, lack of basic skills **139**.17

school leaving age **139**.1, 26

to reduce teenage pregnancies **182**.31

schools

abortion information **171**.36-9

absences, gender differences **154**.25

academies **139**.14-16

anti-bullying policies **165**.1, 8, 25

attendance during pregnancy **182**.6

biometric fingerprinting **168**.30

and CCTV **168**.25

citizenship teaching **131**.36

costs **160**.16-17, 18, 19

and cyberbullying **165**.24-7, 29

and drugs **163**.28-9

and disabled children **197**.5, 23

children with learning problems **197**.14-15

and emergency planning **147**.31-2

and ethnic minority children **115**.18, 19-21

exclusions, gender differences **154**.24

faith-based **148**.34, 35-6

and financial education **180**.38-9

and global citizenship **131**.37

and homophobia **153**.14-18

intake, effect on attainment **149**.31-3

and integration **115**.29, 33

intelligent design, teaching **148**.39

journeys to **119**.25, 26-7, 29-30

and mental health education **141**.37

multi-faith **148**.32-3

and physical activity **162**.13

private, and university entrance **149**.34-5

and physical activity **162**.13

pupil-teacher ratio **139**.12

and racism **115**.9, 19-20

self-harm support **199**.5-6

sex education *see* sex education

and sexual health services **182**.31

single-sex **139**.11-12

and special educational needs **197**.14-15, 23

sports, Olympic-style competition **198**.5

statistics **139**.1

and stress **100**.1; **176**.37, 38-9

support for children with suicidal feelings **199**.31, 33

Volume numbers appear first (in bold) followed by page numbers; a change in volume number is preceded by a semi-**colon.**

Vol. 88 Food and Nutrition

Vol. 97 Energy Matters

Vol. 99 Exploited Children

Vol. 100 Stress and Anxiety

Vol. 119 Transport Trends

Vol. 129 Gambling Trends

Vol. 134 Customers and Consumerism

Vol. 138 A Genetically Modified Future?

Vol. 139 The Education Problem

Vol. 140 Vegetarian and Vegan Diets

Vol. 141 Mental Health

Vol. 142 Media Issues

Vol. 144 The Cloning Debate

Vol. 146 Sustainability and Environment

Vol. 147 The Terrorism Problem

Vol. 148 Religious Beliefs

Vol. 149 A Classless Society?

Vol. 150 Migration and Population

Vol. 151 Climate Change

Vol. 152 Euthanasia and the Right to Die

Vol. 153 Sexual Orientation and Society

Vol. 154 The Gender Gap

Vol. 155 Domestic Abuse

Vol. 156 Travel and Tourism

Vol. 157 The Problem of Globalisation

Vol. 158 The Internet Revolution

Vol. 159 An Ageing Population

Vol. 160 Poverty and Exclusion

Vol. 161 Waste Issues

Vol. 162 Staying Fit

Vol. 163 Drugs in the UK

Vol. 164 The AIDS Crisis

Vol. 165 Bullying Issues

Vol. 166 Marriage and Cohabitation

Vol. 167 Our Human Rights

Vol. 168 Privacy and Surveillance

Vol. 169 The Animal Rights Debate

Vol. 170 Body Image and Self-Esteem

Vol. 171 Abortion – Rights and Ethics

Vol. 172 Racial and Ethnic Discrimination

Vol. 173 Sexual Health

Vol. 174 Selling Sex

Vol. 175 Citizenship and Participation

Vol. 176 Health Issues for Young People

Vol. 177 Crime in the UK

Vol. 178 Reproductive Ethics

Vol. 179 Tackling Child Abuse

Vol. 180 Money and Finances

Vol. 181 The Housing Issue

Vol. 182 Teenage Conceptions

Vol. 183 Work and Employment

Vol. 184 Understanding Eating Disorders

Vol. 185 Student Matters

Vol. 186 Cannabis Use

Vol. 187 Health and the State

Vol. 188 Tobacco and Health

Vol. 189 The Homeless Population

Vol. 190 Coping with Depression

Vol. 191 The Changing Family

Vol. 192 Bereavement and Grief

Vol. 193 Endangered Species

Vol. 194 Responsible Drinking

Vol. 195 Alternative Medicine

Vol. 196 Censorship Issues

Vol. 197 Living with Disability

Vol. 198 Sport and Society

Vol. 199 Self-Harming and Suicide

and university entrance 149.34-5
vocational courses 183.31
weighing children 162.16
workforce, gender differences 154.25
young people and stress 100.1
see also education; National Curriculum; primary schools;
secondary schools
Schools Councils UK 131.34
science education
A-level choices 139.21-2
gender differences 154.22-3
scientific research, and animal experiments 169.14-26
Scotland
biodiversity threats 146.21
children and gambling 129.32-3
drug assessment for NHS use 187.23
and euthanasia legislation 152.17, 29, 30
feelings of Scottish identity 131.5
health service 187.30
homelessness 189.3
life on the streets 189.18-20
red squirrels 193.37
reintroduction of animals 193.33-4
suicides 199.26
teenage abortions 182.2
teenage pregnancy 182.2, 7
Scotland, Church of and ethics of human cloning 144.5-6
scratchcards and under 16s 129.12
scriptures 148.1
sea level rise 151.8; 157.2
seafood, sustainable 146.29
search engines 158.2, 25-6
Seasonal Affective Disorder (SAD) 141.35; 190.2, 6-7, 22
second-hand goods, consumer rights 134.2
second-hand smoke *see* passive smoking
secondary schools
curriculum 139.5-6
see also A-levels; GCSEs; schools
secondment 183.18
Secret Intelligence Service (MI6) 147.2
secret self and self-harm 199.11
security, national 147.2-3
security alerts 147.30
Security Service (MI5) 147.2
SED-NOS (sleep eating disorder) 184.8
segregation 115.28-32
segregation indices 115.31-2
selective breeding 138.12
Selective Serotonin Re-uptake Inhibitors (SSRIs) 190.10,
32-3
and suicide 190.24
selenium
in red meat 140.12
and vegetarian diets 140.7
self-acceptance 170.8-9
self-affirmation 170.38; 199.6
self-blame *see* blame, feelings of
self build projects 181.30-31
self-directed violence *see* self-harm; suicide
self-employment, graduates 185.30
self-esteem 170.1-16

assessing your self-esteem 170.4-5
and body image 170.19
changes over lifetime 170.16
children 170.9-10
damaging experiences 170.8
definition 170.1-2
effects of bullying 165.16
high, problems of 170.13
improving 170.1, 2, 3, 8-9
children 170.9-10
questionnaire 170.4-5
sources of 170.8
and sport 170.39
self-harm 176.30, 33-5; 190.28-9; 199.1-19
avoidance techniques 199.5-6, 7, 8
case studies 199.9
and depression 190.23
definition 199.1, 4, 20
effects 199.11
minimizing damage 199.7
prevalence 199.4
reasons 199.2, 5, 10-12
risk factors 199.4
risk groups 199.1-2, 4-5
sources of help 199.2-3, 5
self-help 199.2, 5-6, 7, 8
and suicide 199.12, 23-4
treatment 199.13-14, 15
young people 176.33-5
self help housing 181.32
self-image *see* body image
self-loathing as cause of self-harm 199.10
self management training and bipolar disorder 190.11
self-perception 170.11-12
self-poisoning, emergency treatment 199.14
self-reflection 170.12
semantic web 158.25-6
semen and fertility problems 178.4-5
sensory impairment and age 159.4
sentencing 177.24-6
community sentencing 177.24, 25-9
knife crime 177.38-9
youth courts 177.17-18
separation
effect on children 166.4-5, 29-31, 32; 191.1, 9
see also divorce
separatism, Islam 147.18
serotonin 141.9
services and child labour 99.2, 4
sex
and cannabis use 186.29
definition 154.1
and the Internet 196.36-9
sex discrimination 154.6
in the workplace 154.30
see also glass ceiling, pay gap
worldwide 154.13-14
sex education 182.28-9, 32-5
and magazines 142.28, 29
role of parents 182.34-5
sex offenders

disclosure of **179**.20-21
help for **179**.22-3
sex offenders notification **177**.18
travel restriction **156**.37
sex stereotyping *see* gender stereotyping
sex tourism **156**.37-9
sexist bullying **165**.9, 10-11, 12-14
sexual abuse **179**.2-3, 13-29
and child domestic workers **99**.8, 9
effects **179**.24-5
false memories **179**.26-9
getting help **179**.25
and the Internet **179**.15-17
of older people **159**.16-17
signs of **179**.5
statistics **179**.13, 15, 17
and stress **100**.1, 2
sexual abusers *see* paedophiles; sex offenders
sexual behaviour
and alcohol **194**.19, 23
and HIV **96**.12, 14, 16, 17
and sexually transmitted infections **96**.9, 12
teenagers **182**.1
sexual exploitation of children **99**.1, 4, 16-18, 20-8; **167**.22
case studies **99**.21-2
harmful effects of **99**.16, 20
and poverty **99**.16, 24
and sex tourism **156**.37-9
teenagers **99**.20-2
and trafficking **99**.3, 16, 17, 18, 20, 21, 24, 28
see also child pornography; child prostitution
sexual health **176**.21-8
being ready for sex **176**.21-2
and cannabis use **186**.29
and migrants **150**.21-3
safe sex **176**.22, 27, 28
sexual dysfunction **176**.23
see also contraception; sexually transmitted infections
sexual health services in schools **182**.31
sexual identity confusion **149**.5
sexual offences prevention order **177**.18
sexual orientation **153**.1-25

and bullying **165**.2, 9, 12-14
causes **153**.2, 6, 7
definition **153**.1
discovering **153**.1-2, 4, 7, 12
and eating disorders in men **184**.13
and the law **153**.26-39
modification therapy **153**.3
prejudice **153**.2-3
survey **153**.5
sexual rights **196**.36
threats to **196**.38
sexualisation
media influence **196**.25-6
of young girls **154**.10
sexuality *see* sexual orientation
sexually transmitted infections (STIs) **96**.1-13; **176**.23, 24-8
avoiding **96**.1-2; **176**.24, 26
bacterial **96**.3, 10, 12
chlamydia **96**.2-3, 4, 5, 8, 10, 12; **176**.25, 26
effects on fertility **178**.5
genital herpes **96**.3, 4, 6, 10, 12
genital warts **96**.2-3, 4, 5-6, 12-13
gonorrhoea **96**.2, 3, 4, 5, 8, 10, 12
and HIV **96**.10, 12, 25
increase in **96**.4
pubic lice **96**.7
and sexual behaviour **96**.9, 12
symptoms of **96**.1, 5, 6, 7
syphilis **96**.3, 4, 6, 8, 10, 12
testing for **96**.1, 2, 3, 5, 6, 7, 10
treatment of **96**.1, 5, 6, 7, 10
trichomonas vaginalis **96**.6-7
types of **96**.2
in the UK **96**.2-3, 4
viral **96**.12-13
and young people **96**.3, 4, 8-9; **176**.25, 26, 28
see also Genito-Urinary Medicine (GUM) clinics
shared accommodation, and planning policy **181**.19-20
shared ownership homes **181**.25, 31
sheep-goat chimera (geep) **144**.10
Shelter **189**.25, 30, 34
shoes, recycling **161**.28

Volume numbers appear first (in bold) followed by page numbers; a change in volume number is preceded by a semi-**colon**.

Vol. 88 Food and Nutrition
Vol. 97 Energy Matters
Vol. 99 Exploited Children
Vol. 100 Stress and Anxiety
Vol. 119 Transport Trends
Vol. 129 Gambling Trends
Vol. 134 Customers and Consumerism
Vol. 138 A Genetically Modified Future?
Vol. 139 The Education Problem
Vol. 140 Vegetarian and Vegan Diets
Vol. 141 Mental Health
Vol. 142 Media Issues
Vol. 144 The Cloning Debate
Vol. 146 Sustainability and Environment
Vol. 147 The Terrorism Problem
Vol. 148 Religious Beliefs
Vol. 149 A Classless Society?
Vol. 150 Migration and Population
Vol. 151 Climate Change
Vol. 152 Euthanasia and the Right to Die
Vol. 153 Sexual Orientation and Society
Vol. 154 The Gender Gap
Vol. 155 Domestic Abuse

Vol. 156 Travel and Tourism
Vol. 157 The Problem of Globalisation
Vol. 158 The Internet Revolution
Vol. 159 An Ageing Population
Vol. 160 Poverty and Exclusion
Vol. 161 Waste Issues
Vol. 162 Staying Fit
Vol. 163 Drugs in the UK
Vol. 164 The AIDS Crisis
Vol. 165 Bullying Issues
Vol. 166 Marriage and Cohabitation
Vol. 167 Our Human Rights
Vol. 168 Privacy and Surveillance
Vol. 169 The Animal Rights Debate
Vol. 170 Body Image and Self-Esteem
Vol. 171 Abortion – Rights and Ethics
Vol. 172 Racial and Ethnic Discrimination
Vol. 173 Sexual Health
Vol. 174 Selling Sex
Vol. 175 Citizenship and Participation
Vol. 176 Health Issues for Young People
Vol. 177 Crime in the UK
Vol. 178 Reproductive Ethics

Vol. 179 Tackling Child Abuse
Vol. 180 Money and Finances
Vol. 181 The Housing Issue
Vol. 182 Teenage Conceptions
Vol. 183 Work and Employment
Vol. 184 Understanding Eating Disorders
Vol. 185 Student Matters
Vol. 186 Cannabis Use
Vol. 187 Health and the State
Vol. 188 Tobacco and Health
Vol. 189 The Homeless Population
Vol. 190 Coping with Depression
Vol. 191 The Changing Family
Vol. 192 Bereavement and Grief
Vol. 193 Endangered Species
Vol. 194 Responsible Drinking
Vol. 195 Alternative Medicine
Vol. 196 Censorship Issues
Vol. 197 Living with Disability
Vol. 198 Sport and Society
Vol. 199 Self-Harming and Suicide

shopping
    addiction to **134**.13, 14
    and animal welfare **140**.31, 33
    and children **134**.12
    and energy efficiency **97**.31-2
    Internet **134**.15-16; **158**.3, 30-31
    as social experience for women **134**.16
    see also consumer rights; consumerism; consumers
shouting as form of child abuse **179**.39
siblings
    donor siblings **178**.26-7
    saviour siblings **178**.28-31
Sicari (early Jewish terrorists) **147**.4
sickness absence **154**.18; **183**.8, 9
    due to smoking **188**.22
    going to work when sick **183**.9
Siemens Generation21 initiative **139**.22
Sikhism **148**.5
    and faith schools **148**.35
    festivals **148**.5
    food rules **148**.5
    funerals **192**.35
simple carbohydrates **88**.2
single parents *see* lone parents
single-sex education **139**.11-12; **154**.25, 26, 27
single-sex youth work **154**.5
Sites of Special Scientific Interest (SSSIs) **146**.32
SIV (self-inflicted violence) *see* self-harm
size-related bullying **165**.8-9
size zero **170**.20; **184**.23
skin cancer **176**.10-11
skunk (cannabis) **186**.9, 11
    mental health effects **186**.13
Sky and environmentalism **146**.38
slander **142**.26
slavery **167**.20-22
    Britain **167**.21, 22
    children **99**.1; **167**.32-3
    statistics **167**.20
sleep
    and exercise **141**.39
    and mental health **141**.34
    and stress **100**.19, 27, 29
sleep eating disorder (SED-NOS) **184**.8
sleeping rough *see* rough sleeping
slum tours **156**.33-5
smacking children **167**.36-9
    arguments against ban **167**.39; **179**.33
    and human rights **167**.36-8; **179**.30, 31-2
    public opinion **179**.32
    see also corporal punishment
smallpox vaccinations **147**.31
smokeless tobacco **188**.11
smoking **188**.1-38
    age of starting smoking **188**.3
    and cancer **188**.8-11
    cannabis *see* cannabis
    children **176**.3, 12-13
        and the law **176**.13
        starting smoking **176**.12
    costs of **188**.15, 22-3

    as deterrent **176**.13
    deaths from **163**.11
    effects on appearance **176**.11
        concerns of young people **188**.14
    effects on fertility **178**.5
    giving up **188**.6, 13-14, 17
        benefits **188**.6, 9
        pregnant women **188**.30-32
        reasons for giving up **188**.13
        tips on giving up **188**.13-14, 16
    and health **188**.5-12, 15, 18, 19, 22
        benefits of giving up **188**.6, 9
        children **176**.12-13
        passive smoking **188**.5, 10-11, 12
        in pregnancy **188**.11, 31
    imagery influencing young people **188**.24-6
    and life expectancy **188**.18
    men **188**.1, 3
        effects of smoking 15
    passive smoking **188**.5, 10-11, 12
    and pregnancy **182**.15; **188**.11, 30-32
    prevalence **188**.1-3
    pro-smoking views **188**.34-5
    and stress **100**.19, 27, 31, 34, 35, 37
    students **185**.9
    women **188**.1, 3
        effects of smoking **188**.15
        pregnant women **182**.15; **188**.11, 30-32
    young people **176**.4, 12-13
        influences on smoking habits **188**.24-8
        prevention **176**.13
        stopping smoking **188**.13-14
smuggling
    drugs **163**.37-8
    tobacco **188**.23
snuff **188**.11
social care services
    and older people **159**.4, 28, 26, 29
social class **149**.1-17
    and advertising **134**.8
    and alcohol consumption, teenagers **194**.24
    and attitudes to money **149**.19-20
    and attitudes to moving home **149**.26
    and children's nutrition **162**.13-14
    classification **149**.3, 5
    confusion over **149**.4
    and educational attainment **149**.30, 31-3; **154**.23
    gender and pupil behaviour **154**.24-5
    and mental health problems **141**.2
    and obesity **162**.5
    psychology of **149**.6
    regional differences **149**.18
    self-awareness of **149**.3, 4, 18, 19, 24
    see also social mobility
social and cultural globalisation **157**.2
social differences, children's perceptions of **149**.9-12
social drinking **194**.17
social exclusion
    and education **160**.17-18
    older people **159**.30
social factors

and gambling **129**.7, 29

and suicide **199**.24

social gambling **129**.11, 18

social group classification system **149**.3, 5

social housing

attitudes to **181**.14

and children **181**.9-11

demand for **181**.29

effects of **181**.9-11; 33-5

and immigrants **181**.12

quality **181**.10

shortage **181**.8

social identity theory and football support **141**.32-3

social isolation

Asians **115**.37

older people **159**.3, 8, 17, 30

social marketing

and reducing consumption **161**.34

and sex education **182**.39

social mobility **160**.7

and education **139**.13; **149**.22, 25, 30, 36-7

and higher education **185**.18

international comparisons **149**.25

and the profession **185**.38-9

social model of disability **197**.2

social networking **142**.35, 36, 38; **158**.3, 9

and globalisation **157**.15

and mobile phones **158**.11-12

and privacy **168**.34-6

safety **158**.9, 10-11; **179**.18

and travel **156**.14

and workplace bullying **165**.37-8

social pessimism **177**.1-4

social problems, public perceptions of **177**.1-4

social profiles by neighbourhood **149**.17, 23

social responsibility, corporate **157**.11

social roles and gender differences **154**.9

social security benefits *see* state benefits

social skills gap **149**.37-8

social status and ageing **159**.32

social topography **149**.17, 23

social workers

and stress in young people **100**.2

and workplace stress **100**.12

socio-economic deprivation, migrants **150**.22

socio-economic groups

and life expectancy **188**.18

and news awareness **142**.31

and obesity **162**.5

and smoking **188**.2, 3, 33

see also social class

sofa surfing **189**.7

soft segregation **115**.28

soft skills (emotional skills) **170**.5

Soil Association standards

free-range eggs **140**.29, 39

organic farming **140**.35

soil management **88**.14

solar activity and global warming **151**.5-6

solar energy **97**.2, 4, 6, 8-9, 10, 21

costs of **97**.14

and energy efficiency **97**.31

market for **97**.14

PV (Photovoltaics) **97**.8, 9, 12, 13, 38

in the UK **97**.10, 13, 14, 26

soldiers, child *see* child soldiers

solicitors

and divorce **166**.35

and mediation **166**.39

solid fuels, as a source of energy **97**.4

solvent abuse **163**.5-6

deaths from **163**.11

somatic-cell nuclear transfer (SCNT) **144**.1-2, 9, 26

see also therapeutic cloning

souvenirs, wildlife **156**.32

Soviet Union **157**.7

Starbucks and anti-globalisation campaigns **157**.30

Soweto township tours **156**.35

soya products for vegetarians **140**.22, 23, 26

spa holidays 5

space

as a natural resource **146**.9

sustainable use of **146**.17

Spain, bullfighting **169**.37-9

Volume numbers appear first (in bold) followed by page numbers; a change in volume number is preceded by a semi-**colon.**

Vol. 88 Food and Nutrition
Vol. 97 Energy Matters
Vol. 99 Exploited Children
Vol. 100 Stress and Anxiety
Vol. 119 Transport Trends
Vol. 129 Gambling Trends
Vol. 134 Customers and Consumerism
Vol. 138 A Genetically Modified Future?
Vol. 139 The Education Problem
Vol. 140 Vegetarian and Vegan Diets
Vol. 141 Mental Health
Vol. 142 Media Issues
Vol. 144 The Cloning Debate
Vol. 146 Sustainability and Environment
Vol. 147 The Terrorism Problem
Vol. 148 Religious Beliefs
Vol. 149 A Classless Society?
Vol. 150 Migration and Population
Vol. 151 Climate Change
Vol. 152 Euthanasia and the Right to Die
Vol. 153 Sexual Orientation and Society
Vol. 154 The Gender Gap
Vol. 155 Domestic Abuse

Vol. 156 Travel and Tourism
Vol. 157 The Problem of Globalisation
Vol. 158 The Internet Revolution
Vol. 159 An Ageing Population
Vol. 160 Poverty and Exclusion
Vol. 161 Waste Issues
Vol. 162 Staying Fit
Vol. 163 Drugs in the UK
Vol. 164 The AIDS Crisis
Vol. 165 Bullying Issues
Vol. 166 Marriage and Cohabitation
Vol. 167 Our Human Rights
Vol. 168 Privacy and Surveillance
Vol. 169 The Animal Rights Debate
Vol. 170 Body Image and Self-Esteem
Vol. 171 Abortion – Rights and Ethics
Vol. 172 Racial and Ethnic Discrimination
Vol. 173 Sexual Health
Vol. 174 Selling Sex
Vol. 175 Citizenship and Participation
Vol. 176 Health Issues for Young People
Vol. 177 Crime in the UK
Vol. 178 Reproductive Ethics

Vol. 179 Tackling Child Abuse
Vol. 180 Money and Finances
Vol. 181 The Housing Issue
Vol. 182 Teenage Conceptions
Vol. 183 Work and Employment
Vol. 184 Understanding Eating Disorders
Vol. 185 Student Matters
Vol. 186 Cannabis Use
Vol. 187 Health and the State
Vol. 188 Tobacco and Health
Vol. 189 The Homeless Population
Vol. 190 Coping with Depression
Vol. 191 The Changing Family
Vol. 192 Bereavement and Grief
Vol. 193 Endangered Species
Vol. 194 Responsible Drinking
Vol. 195 Alternative Medicine
Vol. 196 Censorship Issues
Vol. 197 Living with Disability
Vol. 198 Sport and Society
Vol. 199 Self-Harming and Suicide

Special Areas of Conservation 146.33
Special Educational Needs (SEN) 197.14-15, 23
    gender differences 154.24
specialist diplomas 139.23-5
species boundaries 144.12
species loss 193.13
    England 193.31-2
    Galapagos Islands 193.24-5
Species Recovery Programme 146.33
species reintroduction, Britain 193.33-4
specific issue order 166.27, 35
spectacles, recycling 161.28
speech pathologists 197.4
speed cameras 119.4, 17, 18
speed limiters 119.18
speed limits
    and active traffic management 119.37-8
    raising 119.4
speeding 119.3, 4, 8
    and pedestrian injuries 119.5, 30-31
spending 134.3-4; 180.7
    on advertising 134.7
    and budgeting 180.30-31
    on credit cards 134.24
    on education 139.1
    on ethical products 134.31, 32
    older people 159.19
    on tourism 156.5, 10
    see also consumer spending
sperm cell creation
    from bone marrow 144.29
    from stem cells 178.39
sperm donation 178.10-12
    concerns about 178.12
    donor contact with offspring 178.25-7
    effects of removing donor anonymity 178.24
spiking drinks 194.8-10
spin doctors 131.18
spina bifida 197.3
spinal damage, stem cell therapy 144.21
spirituality 148.1
    interest in 148.19
sport 198.1-39
    betting 129.2
    and drugs see drugs in sport
    and inclusion 198.18-26
    and self-esteem 170.39
    trends 198.1-17
Sport England, funding for disability sport 198.18
spot-reduction of fat 162.33
spread betting 129.2
spyware 158.34
    and domestic abuse 155.15-16
squatting 181.20
squirrels
    grey 193.38
    red, Scotland 193.37
SSRIs (Selective Serotonin Re-Uptake Inhibitors) 190.10, 32-3
stamp duty 181.24
    political party policies 181.23

standing orders 180.14
Staphylococcus aureus 88.29
starchy foods 88.5-6, 12
state benefits 160.23-4
    after bereavement 192.30-31, 32
    costs of incapacity benefit 100.23
    disabled people 197.31-4
    jobseekers' allowance 100.23
    maternity pay 191.38
    and migrants 150.7
    and National Identity Scheme 168.16, 18
    see also disability benefits
state pension 159.3, 23
state religion 148.21-2
statements of special education needs 197.23
statutory homelessness 189.3-4
Statutory Maternity Pay 191.38
steel cans recycling 161.27
stem cell lines 144.18
    personalized 144.25
stem cell research 144.2, 15-29; 178.38
    embryonic 178.33-7
    ethical issues 144.6, 17; 178.33-5
    how it works 144.16
    humanist view 178.36-7
    induced pluripotent stem cells 178.38
    public attitudes to 138.16; 144.19
    timeline 144.27-8, 33
    using hybrid embryos 144.14
stem cell therapy 144.17-18, 21-6, 28
stem cell transplants, saviour siblings 178.28-31
stem cells 144.15, 17-18
    from bone marrow 144.21, 23
stepfamilies 191.10
sterile-seed (Terminator) technology 138.18
sterilization 182.19
    and fertility 178.4
steroids see anabolic agents/steroids
STIs see sexually transmitted infections
stimulants (uppers) 163.2, 4-5
    and sports drug abuse 198.29
    see also amphetamines; cocaine; ecstasy
Stop Huntingdon Animal Cruelty (SHAC) 147.21
stop and search 147.35-7; 177.34
stopping cannabis use 186.11
stopping smoking see smoking, giving up
store cards 134.22; 180.14, 26
    and personal data 168.8
storms, and climate change 151.8
Strategic Health Authorities 187.5
stratosphere cooling 151.4
street children 99.1, 18-19
    as tourist sights 156.33-4
street crime 177.4-5
street fighting 177.5
street homelessness 189.18-20
    young people 189.27-8
stress
    avoiding 141.36
    and anxiety 100.2, 21
    coping with 100.27-39

defining **100**.1, 5, 33
and exams **176**.5, 38-9
and exercise **141**.39; **162**.37
factors determining degree of **100**.14-15
and fertility **178**.5
'fight or flight' response to **100**.1, 14-15, 25, 28
harmful effects of **100**.28, 38
health benefits of the right sort of **100**.39
in laboratory animals **169**.16, 21
and lifestyle **100**.19, 31-2
positive and negative **100**.14
school stress **176**.37, 38-9
signs and symptoms of **100**.1, 2, 5, 12, 28-9, 33, 35
statistics on **100**.13, 19
stay-at-home parents **191**.35
work-related **165**.34
   costs **183**.6-7
stress management **100**.32, 36
strokes **159**.4
   stem cell therapy **144**.22
structural adjustment **157**.7
students
accommodation **181**.18, 19-20; **185**.7
applying to university **139**.29-32
   and parental educational level **149**.7, 31, 35
health issues **176**.5-6
housing **185**.7
living at home **149**.2
mental health **185**.8
and money matters **134**.24; **139**.34-5; **180**.28-9, 32-3
   budgeting **180**.30-31; **185**.3, 11
   costs of a university education **139**.34, 35; **185**.11, 17, 36
   graduate starting salaries **139**.35, 36; **185**.33-4
   grants **180**.28, 33; **185**.2
   income and expenditure **180**.32-3
   loans **139**.34; **180**.28, 33; **185**.2
   part-time work **139**.35
from overseas, entry allowed **150**.23
satisfaction with course **185**.4-5
statistics **139**.2, 32
student life **185**.3-4

and terrorism **147**.13-14
study leave **183**.18
substance abuse
and depression **190**.3
and homelessness **189**.10-11
see also alcohol; drug abuse; solvent abuse
suburban aspirations **149**.26
suction aspiration (abortion) **171**.2
suffering, animals
and animal experiments **169**.14-15, 16, 25
animal transport **169**.10
emotional **169**.2
fur farming **169**.5
intensively farmed chickens **169**.13
suicidal feelings **199**.23
and bullying **165**.20, 21-2
children **176**.35, 36-7
getting help **199**.20, 22, 28
how to help someone **199**.22, 25-6, 30, 32-3
reasons **199**.20, 24, 30
young people **190**.29
suicide **199**.20-39
and anti-depressants **190**.24
copycat suicides **199**.36
and depression **190**.21, 23
and the Internet **199**.33, 35
and the media **142**.30; **199**.35, 36
myths **199**.27
reasons for **199**.24, 30
risk factors for **199**.20-21, 31-2
risk groups **199**.20-21, 24-5
and self-harm **199**.12, 23-4
statistics **190**.27; **199**.21
support for suicidal people **199**.20, 22, 26, 30
   children **199**.33
   men **199**.38
   Samaritans **199**.20, 22, 31, 35
warning signs **190**.26-7; **199**.22, 25, 29-30, 31-2
young people **190**.26, 27; **199**.21, 31-3
see also assisted suicide; attempted suicide; physician-assisted suicide (PAS)
sulphur dioxide (SO₂) emissions **119**.15; **146**.35

Volume numbers appear first (in bold) followed by page numbers; a change in volume number is preceded by a semi-**colon.**

Vol. 88 Food and Nutrition
Vol. 97 Energy Matters
Vol. 99 Exploited Children
Vol. 100 Stress and Anxiety
Vol. 119 Transport Trends
Vol. 129 Gambling Trends
Vol. 134 Customers and Consumerism
Vol. 138 A Genetically Modified Future?
Vol. 139 The Education Problem
Vol. 140 Vegetarian and Vegan Diets
Vol. 141 Mental Health
Vol. 142 Media Issues
Vol. 144 The Cloning Debate
Vol. 146 Sustainability and Environment
Vol. 147 The Terrorism Problem
Vol. 148 Religious Beliefs
Vol. 149 A Classless Society?
Vol. 150 Migration and Population
Vol. 151 Climate Change
Vol. 152 Euthanasia and the Right to Die
Vol. 153 Sexual Orientation and Society
Vol. 154 The Gender Gap
Vol. 155 Domestic Abuse

Vol. 156 Travel and Tourism
Vol. 157 The Problem of Globalisation
Vol. 158 The Internet Revolution
Vol. 159 An Ageing Population
Vol. 160 Poverty and Exclusion
Vol. 161 Waste Issues
Vol. 162 Staying Fit
Vol. 163 Drugs in the UK
Vol. 164 The AIDS Crisis
Vol. 165 Bullying Issues
Vol. 166 Marriage and Cohabitation
Vol. 167 Our Human Rights
Vol. 168 Privacy and Surveillance
Vol. 169 The Animal Rights Debate
Vol. 170 Body Image and Self-Esteem
Vol. 171 Abortion – Rights and Ethics
Vol. 172 Racial and Ethnic Discrimination
Vol. 173 Sexual Health
Vol. 174 Selling Sex
Vol. 175 Citizenship and Participation
Vol. 176 Health Issues for Young People
Vol. 177 Crime in the UK
Vol. 178 Reproductive Ethics

Vol. 179 Tackling Child Abuse
Vol. 180 Money and Finances
Vol. 181 The Housing Issue
Vol. 182 Teenage Conceptions
Vol. 183 Work and Employment
Vol. 184 Understanding Eating Disorders
Vol. 185 Student Matters
Vol. 186 Cannabis Use
Vol. 187 Health and the State
Vol. 188 Tobacco and Health
Vol. 189 The Homeless Population
Vol. 190 Coping with Depression
Vol. 191 The Changing Family
Vol. 192 Bereavement and Grief
Vol. 193 Endangered Species
Vol. 194 Responsible Drinking
Vol. 195 Alternative Medicine
Vol. 196 Censorship Issues
Vol. 197 Living with Disability
Vol. 198 Sport and Society
Vol. 199 Self-Harming and Suicide

summer depression **190**.7
sunbeds and cancer **176**.10-11
superbugs, hospital **187**.28-9
supercasinos **129**.14-16, 34
supermarkets
    and Fairtrade **134**.36
    and free-range eggs **140**.38
    and GM products **138**.26
    impact on communities **134**.38
    packaging waste **161**.12
    and plastic bags **161**.13-14
    and vegetarianism **140**.20
supervision orders **177**.17, 26
support groups
    domestic abuse perpetrators **155**.33-4
    domestic abuse sufferers **155**.6-7, 28-9
    gamblers **129**.37
    sexual abusers **179**.22-3
surgery, weight loss **162**.3
surgical abortion **171**.2
surname choice of women **154**.19-20
surrogacy **178**.7-8, 13-14
    and parents' rights **153**.34
    and same-sex couples **178**.10
    success rate **178**.14
surveillance **147**.29
    by the government **168**.4-5, 7-8, 13-14, 27, 35
    and law **168**.10-11
    by local authorities **168**.20-21
    online **168**.32-3
    risks **168**.4
    by satellite **168**.26-7
suspended sentence orders **177**.26
sustainability **146**.1-11
    construction industry **146**.11
    consumption **146**.7, 8
    definition **146**.3
    fossil fuels **151**.28-30
    Millennium Development Goals **160**.32
    production **146**.7, 8
    seafood **146**.29
    UK principles **146**.3
    UK strategy **146**.8-9
sustainable agriculture **88**.32-3; **146**.27
sustainable communities **146**.9
Sustainable Development Strategy **146**.8-9
sustainable housing **181**.39
sustainable population **150**.31-2
sustainable tourism **156**.8, 22-3, 24
    attitudes to **156**.29-30
sustainable use of space **146**.17
swearing on television **196**.21
sweatshops **157**.27-9
sweepstake scams **134**.26
swimming, funding cuts **198**.6-7
Switzerland, assisted suicide **152**.18, 19

T

t-GURTS **138**.18

tabloid newspapers **142**.8
tactile warning devices, cars **119**.19
talent identification
    Olympic sports **198**.8-10
    Paralympic sports **198**.22
talking
    about dying **192**.8, 24
    about feelings **141**.34
    and the grieving process **192**.5
    see also communication
talking therapies **141**.35; **190**.5, 11, 34
tar, in cigarette smoke **188**.4
    effect on heart **188**.7
    effect on lungs **188**.5
tariffs *see* trade barriers
Tasers **177**.31-2
taxation **180**.24
    after death **192**.32
    on aviation fuel **119**.16
    carbon tax on fuel **97**.25
    and civil partnerships **153**.28
    congestion tax **119**.34
    fuel taxes **119**.14, 24
    gambling **129**.18
    and income inequality **160**.6
    landfill tax **161**.12, 20, 35
    on savings interest **180**.26
    tobacco **188**.23
    and trade **157**.12-13
taxis and disabled people **197**.12
tea, fairtrade **157**.33-4
teachers
    concerns about CCTV in schools **168**.25
    gender gap **154**.25
    homophobic bullying **153**.14, 16, 17
    not encouraging Oxbridge applications 24
    numbers of **139**.1, 12
    salaries **139**.12
    and stress in young people **100**.1
    and workplace stress **100**.12
technological change, and workplace stress **100**.16
teenage depression **190**.25-7, 30
teenage magazines **142**.28
teenage mothers **182**.16
    supervised homes **182**.17-18
teenage parents **182**.14-18
    see also teenage fathers; teenage mothers
teenage pregnancies **176**.4; **182**.1-13
    and abortion **182**.12-13
    options **182**.6, 8-9
    public perceptions of **182**.13
    risks **182**.11, 37
    statistics **182**.2, 7, 10-11, 37
Teenage Pregnancy Strategy **182**.24, 25-6, 27
teenage suicide, warning signs **190**.26-7
teenagers *see* young people
teetotallers **194**.11-12
telecommunications, broadband **158**.5-6
telephones
  communications database **168**.13-14
    competitions **158**.6
    mobile *see* mobile phones

Telephone Preference Service **134**.20, 28
telephone sales and consumer rights **134**.20
television **158**.5
    advertising and children **134**.10, 12
    children's viewing, control of **158**.32
    and homosexuality **153**.23-5
    as news source **142**.33
    offensive language **196**.21, 24
    online **158**.21-2
    reality television, promoting racial understanding **115**.22
    regulation, Ofcom **196**.18-20
    young people's viewing habits **142**.38
teleworking *see* homeworking
telomeres and ageing **159**.32, 33; **162**.12
temperature of the earth
    'hockey stick' graph **151**.15
    measurement errors **151**.4-5
temporary accommodation **189**.8
tenancy sustainment services **189**.34
tenants
    council tenants' rights to move **181**.35-6
    rights **181**.16
terminally ill people
    assisted suicide *see* assisted suicide
    and carer's grief **192**.6
    euthanasia *see* euthanasia
termination *see* abortion
Terminator (sterile-seed) technology **138**.18
terms of trade **157**.7
territorial privacy **168**.2
terrorism **147**.1-25
    countering **147**.26-39
    definition **147**.1, 4
    fear of **147**.12
    history **147**.1, 4-5
    and identity cards **131**.14; **168**.16, 18
    and the Internet **147**.8-9
    and Islamophobia **131**.11
    London bombings **115**.27, 36
    public support for anti-terrorism measures **167**.24
    reaction to **147**.10-11, 38-9
    and satellite surveillance **168**.27

statistics **147**.6
targeting terrorist funds **147**.3, 28-9
Terrorism Acts **147**.3, 27, 35-6
timeline **147**.5
effect on tourism **156**.8
types **147**.1
Tesco and plastic bags **161**.13
test tube babies *see* in vitro fertilisation
testicles and fertility problems **178**.5
tetrahydrocannabinol *see* THC
Tetra Pak cartons, recycling **161**.23
text messages
    bullying **165**.23
    preventing unwanted texts **134**.28
textile industry, working conditions **157**.27-9
textiles recycling **161**.25, 28
textured vegetable protein (TVP) **140**.19
TfST (Time Off for Study or Training) **183**.29
THC (delta-9 tetrahydrocannabinol)
    and cannabis strength **186**.7, 22
    effects **186**.9
    in skunk **186**.13
therapeutic activity **195**.9
therapeutic cloning **144**.2, 15, 16, 26; **178**.34
    embryonic stem cells **144**.25
    humanist view of **144**.7; **178**.36-7
therapeutic use exemption, drugs in sport **198**.28
therapists, complementary **195**.1, 3
    see also complementary and alternative medicine
Third World **157**.7
    see also developing countries
threatened environments as tourist destinations **156**.27
tidal energy **97**.2, 6, 12
tigers, as endangered species **193**.1, 18
timber production **146**.30-31
    environmental impact **193**.4
timber recycling **161**.25
time limit for abortion **171**.29, 30, 31, 32-4
time management, and stress **100**.27, 29, 32, 36
Time Off for Study or Training (TfST) **183**.29
tins, recycling **161**.27
TNCs *see* transnational corporations

Volume numbers appear first (in bold) followed by page numbers; a change in volume number is preceded by a semi-**colon.**

Vol. 88 Food and Nutrition
Vol. 97 Energy Matters
Vol. 99 Exploited Children
Vol. 100 Stress and Anxiety
Vol. 119 Transport Trends
Vol. 129 Gambling Trends
Vol. 134 Customers and Consumerism
Vol. 138 A Genetically Modified Future?
Vol. 139 The Education Problem
Vol. 140 Vegetarian and Vegan Diets
Vol. 141 Mental Health
Vol. 142 Media Issues
Vol. 144 The Cloning Debate
Vol. 146 Sustainability and Environment
Vol. 147 The Terrorism Problem
Vol. 148 Religious Beliefs
Vol. 149 A Classless Society?
Vol. 150 Migration and Population
Vol. 151 Climate Change
Vol. 152 Euthanasia and the Right to Die
Vol. 153 Sexual Orientation and Society
Vol. 154 The Gender Gap
Vol. 155 Domestic Abuse

Vol. 156 Travel and Tourism
Vol. 157 The Problem of Globalisation
Vol. 158 The Internet Revolution
Vol. 159 An Ageing Population
Vol. 160 Poverty and Exclusion
Vol. 161 Waste Issues
Vol. 162 Staying Fit
Vol. 163 Drugs in the UK
Vol. 164 The AIDS Crisis
Vol. 165 Bullying Issues
Vol. 166 Marriage and Cohabitation
Vol. 167 Our Human Rights
Vol. 168 Privacy and Surveillance
Vol. 169 The Animal Rights Debate
Vol. 170 Body Image and Self-Esteem
Vol. 171 Abortion – Rights and Ethics
Vol. 172 Racial and Ethnic Discrimination
Vol. 173 Sexual Health
Vol. 174 Selling Sex
Vol. 175 Citizenship and Participation
Vol. 176 Health Issues for Young People
Vol. 177 Crime in the UK
Vol. 178 Reproductive Ethics

Vol. 179 Tackling Child Abuse
Vol. 180 Money and Finances
Vol. 181 The Housing Issue
Vol. 182 Teenage Conceptions
Vol. 183 Work and Employment
Vol. 184 Understanding Eating Disorders
Vol. 185 Student Matters
Vol. 186 Cannabis Use
Vol. 187 Health and the State
Vol. 188 Tobacco and Health
Vol. 189 The Homeless Population
Vol. 190 Coping with Depression
Vol. 191 The Changing Family
Vol. 192 Bereavement and Grief
Vol. 193 Endangered Species
Vol. 194 Responsible Drinking
Vol. 195 Alternative Medicine
Vol. 196 Censorship Issues
Vol. 197 Living with Disability
Vol. 198 Sport and Society
Vol. 199 Self-Harming and Suicide

tobacco
    advertising ban **188**.23
    chemical contents of smoke **188**.4, 9-10, 15
    deaths **163**.11
    and the economy **188**.22-3
    and pharming of HIV drugs **138**.21-2
    see also smoking
tobacco industry **188**.23
    tobacco pickers' health problems **188**.39
tobacco-specific nitrosamines (TSNAs) **188**.11
Today newspaper **142**.8-9
tofu **140**.6, 20
toilets, lack of in developing countries **146**.14-15
tolerance to drugs **163**.2
tomatoes, genetically modified **138**.14
TOMPS (toxic organic micropollutants) **146**.35-6
tools, recycling **161**.25
torture **167**.25-7
    evidence obtained under torture **167**.27
touch screen software **158**.22-3
tour operators **156**.1, 8-9
tourism
    best and worst sights **156**.6
    and bullfighting **169**.38
    child sex tourism **99**.17, 20, 23, 25-6; **156**.37-9
    and climate change **156**.1, 25, 28-30
    dependency on **156**.21
    effects of **156**.20-39
    environmental impact **156**.20, 21, 22, 25
    gap years **156**.15-19
    industry **156**.8-9
    Internet bookings **156**.1, 13, 14
    statistics **156**.3-4, 7, 10
    trends **156**.1-14
    visits to the UK **156**.3-4, 10, 13
    see also ecotourism; responsible tourism
tourists
    behaviour **156**.31
    unconcerned about environmental impact **156**.28-30
    visiting threatened environments **156**.27
tower blocks and racial segregation **115**.32
toxic chemicals in tobacco smoke **188**.4, 9-10, 15
toxic organic micropollutants (TOMPS) **146**.35-6
trade, international *see* international trade
trade in endangered species **146**.34; **193**.20-21
    ivory trade ban **193**.19
trade in indecent articles **196**.23
Trade Justice Movement **157**.18
trade liberalisation **157**.12, 20
    see also free trade
trade rules **157**.17
    fairness **157**.17-18, 25
    see also World Trade Organisation
trade unions and workplace stress **100**.11, 26
trading standards **88**.38-9
Traditional Herbal Medicines Registration Scheme (THR)
    195.4, 35, 38
traditional medicine **195**.9, 10
    difficulty of regulating **195**.36
traffic *see* road traffic
TRAFFIC (wildlife trade monitoring network) **146**.34

traffic pollution *see* pollution and transport
trafficking **167**.20, 21, 22
    children **99**.1, 3, 4; **167**.32, 34
    EU laws **179**.29
    and the sexual exploitation of children **99**.3, 16, 17, 20, 21, 24, 28
    women **150**.15
trail huntings **169**.34
training
    and age discrimination **159**.9
    effect of recession **183**.2
    opportunities, racial discrimination **115**.14
    and workplace stress **100**.16
    young people **183**.29
trains *see* railways
tranquilizers **194**.9
transgender people **153**.13
    and equality **154**.4
transgenic bacteria **144**.11
transgenic technology *see* genetic modification
transnational corporations (TNCs) **157**.7
    and the environment **157**.10-11
    see also multinational corporations
transport
    census information **150**.36
    and climate change reduction **151**.39
    and disabled people **197**.11-12, 23
    emissions *see* emissions, transport
    and energy efficiency **97**.24, 25, 31
    environmental **134**.30, 32
    live animals **169**.10
    public attitudes to **97**.35, 36
    spending on **134**.4, 25
    trends **119**.1-16, 29-31; **161**.31-2
Transport 2000 **119**.32-3
Transport Innovation Fund **119**.38
transsexualism **149**.5; **153**.13
transvestism **153**.13
trapping animals **193**.1
    for fur **169**.5, 8
travel
    ethical **134**.30
    and terrorism **147**.32
    see also tourism
travel 2.0 sites **156**.14
travel agents **156**.9
Travel Foundation **156**.23
travellers' cheques **180**.13-14
Travellers of Irish Heritage, and education **115**.18
treatment
    bipolar disorder **190**.10-11
    depression **190**.26, 31-9
    eating disorders **184**.6-7, 29-39
    obesity **162**.2-3, 6, 20
        see also weight management
    Seasonal Affective Disorder **190**.6-7
tree planting and carbon offsetting **151**.35
tricyclic antidepressants **190**.10-11, 33
troposphere warming **151**.4
truancy rates **139**.2
tuberculosis and HIV **164**.30

tuition fees, university **185**.11, 17, 29, 36
TVP (textured vegetable protein) **140**.19
12 Step Programme **184**.30
twins, IVF, and health problems **178**.21-2
two-earner families **149**.28
Tylor, E.B. and James Frazer, on religion **148**.12

U

Uganda, human rights abuses **167**.11
UK
    asylum claims **150**.4, 23
    Biodiversity Action Plan **146**.33
    and children's rights **167**.38
    domestic tourisn **156**.10
    ecological debt **146**.4-6
    economy
      benefits from globalisation **157**.1
    competition from overseas **157**.35-6
    endangered species **193**.31-9
    genetically modified crops **138**.2-3, 5, 39
    Human Rights Act **167**.3, 4, 5, 15-18
    income inequality **160**.6, 7
    natural environment conservation **146**.32-3
    NHS provision differences **187**.29-30
    online gambling market **129**.19, 20
    population, ethnic groups **115**.3
    poverty **160**.1-24
    and sustainable development **146**.3, 8-9
    supercasino **129**.14-16
    tourism industry **156**.7-10, 13
    tourist sights **156**.6
    travel abroad **156**.1, 4
UK Youth Parliament **131**.29, 34
umbilical cord
    blood storage **178**.33
    stem cells **178**.28
UN *see* United Nations
unauthorized absence (truancy) **139**.2
underachievement, black pupils **115**.19-21
underage drinking **176**.17-18

see also young people and alcohol
underage gambling **129**.1
    National Lottery **129**.11-13
    online gambling **129**.18, 25
    online poker **129**.25
    Scotland **129**.32-3
undergraduates *see* students
underground travel and disabled people **197**.12
unemployment
    and adult children living with parents **181**.4
    and incapacity benefit **100**.23
    jobseekers allowance (JSA) **100**.23
    and migration **150**.9-10
    and poverty **160**.2
    and social housing **181**.35
    young people **149**.38-9; **183**.37-8
UNICEF, Convention on the Rights of the Child **167**.28-9
union jack **131**.3-4
unions *see* trade unions
unipolar (endogenous) depression **190**.10, 22-3
UNISON **187**.21
United Nations (UN) **157**.8
    and HIV/AIDS **164**.32, 39
    human rights treaties **167**.1
    UN Committee on the Rights of the Child, and corporal punishment **167**.36; **179**.30, 31
    UN Convention on the Rights of the Child **167**.28-9
    UN Environment Programme (UNEP) **193**.10-11, 13
    UN Strategic Drugs Policy Review **186**.38
units of alcohol **176**.15; **194**.4-5, 14
    recommended safe limits **194**.8, 14, 18
Universal Declaration on Human Genome and Human Rights **144**.3
Universal Declaration of Human Rights **167**.8-10, 14
    and privacy **168**.3
universal social pension **159**.24
universities
    admissions and exam stress **100**.7
    application numbers **139**.31, 32
      from state schools **185**.19-20
    Bristol University, workplace travel plan **119**.32-3
    business involvement **185**.34-6

Volume numbers appear first (in bold) followed by page numbers; a change in volume number is preceded by a semi-**colon.**

Vol. 88 Food and Nutrition
Vol. 97 Energy Matters
Vol. 99 Exploited Children
Vol. 100 Stress and Anxiety
Vol. 119 Transport Trends
Vol. 129 Gambling Trends
Vol. 134 Customers and Consumerism
Vol. 138 A Genetically Modified Future?
Vol. 139 The Education Problem
Vol. 140 Vegetarian and Vegan Diets
Vol. 141 Mental Health
Vol. 142 Media Issues
Vol. 144 The Cloning Debate
Vol. 146 Sustainability and Environment
Vol. 147 The Terrorism Problem
Vol. 148 Religious Beliefs
Vol. 149 A Classless Society?
Vol. 150 Migration and Population
Vol. 151 Climate Change
Vol. 152 Euthanasia and the Right to Die
Vol. 153 Sexual Orientation and Society
Vol. 154 The Gender Gap
Vol. 155 Domestic Abuse

Vol. 156 Travel and Tourism
Vol. 157 The Problem of Globalisation
Vol. 158 The Internet Revolution
Vol. 159 An Ageing Population
Vol. 160 Poverty and Exclusion
Vol. 161 Waste Issues
Vol. 162 Staying Fit
Vol. 163 Drugs in the UK
Vol. 164 The AIDS Crisis
Vol. 165 Bullying Issues
Vol. 166 Marriage and Cohabitation
Vol. 167 Our Human Rights
Vol. 168 Privacy and Surveillance
Vol. 169 The Animal Rights Debate
Vol. 170 Body Image and Self-Esteem
Vol. 171 Abortion – Rights and Ethics
Vol. 172 Racial and Ethnic Discrimination
Vol. 173 Sexual Health
Vol. 174 Selling Sex
Vol. 175 Citizenship and Participation
Vol. 176 Health Issues for Young People
Vol. 177 Crime in the UK
Vol. 178 Reproductive Ethics

Vol. 179 Tackling Child Abuse
Vol. 180 Money and Finances
Vol. 181 The Housing Issue
Vol. 182 Teenage Conceptions
Vol. 183 Work and Employment
Vol. 184 Understanding Eating Disorders
Vol. 185 Student Matters
Vol. 186 Cannabis Use
Vol. 187 Health and the State
Vol. 188 Tobacco and Health
Vol. 189 The Homeless Population
Vol. 190 Coping with Depression
Vol. 191 The Changing Family
Vol. 192 Bereavement and Grief
Vol. 193 Endangered Species
Vol. 194 Responsible Drinking
Vol. 195 Alternative Medicine
Vol. 196 Censorship Issues
Vol. 197 Living with Disability
Vol. 198 Sport and Society
Vol. 199 Self-Harming and Suicide

comparing standards **185**.26-8

costs of a university education **139**.34, 35

courses **139**.2, 29, 30, 38-9

discrimination against middle-class applications **149**.7

'dumbing down' accusations **149**.7

fees **139**.34

government policy framework **185**.25

and integration **115**.30

post-qualification admission **139**.16

reasons for not going to university **185**.16-17

school background of students **149**.34-5; **185**.19-20

selection and parental education **149**.7, 31, 35

and social class **149**.1-2

and social mobility **185**.18-20

student finance **180**.28-9, 32-3

university structure reform **185**.20-21

see also degrees; further education; students

upbringing and gender development **154**.1

uppers *see* stimulants

urban areas and climate change **151**.10-12

urban growth **146**.17, 24

urbanisation **150**.33, 35, 37-8

urine testing in sport **198**.27

USA

attitudes to religion **148**.19

criticism of NHS **187**.19-20

environmental impact **193**.5

and euthanasia **152**.4, 18, 19, 31, 33

gambling **129**.27

underage online poker **129**.25

and GM crops **138**.27

human rights abuses **167**.23

lifting funding ban on pro-abortion groups **171**.13-14

and mixed-race relationships **115**.24

privacy rights **168**.3

USSR **157**.7

utilitarian drug use **163**.1

V

v-GURTs **138**.18

vaccination

and organic farming **140**.35-6

search for AIDS vaccine **164**.34-6

vacuum aspiration (abortion) **171**.2

value for money, and consumer rights **134**.2

values

and Britishness **131**.1

human **148**.15

religious **148**.16

vascular dementia **141**.6

VCE (Vocational Certificate of Education) **139**.18

veganism **140**.2, 7, 25-6

costs of **140**.25

and health **140**.25

and protein **140**.23-4

and restaurants **140**.25

VegeMince **140**.19

vegetables *see* fruit and vegetables

vegetarian diets **140**.2, 6, 7

vegetarianism **88**.18; **140**.1-26

definition **140**.1, 5

eating out **140**.5, 25

and food ingredients **140**.18

number of vegetarians **140**.20, 39

reasons for becoming vegetarian **140**.1, 5, 8, 14

and supermarkets **140**.20

Vehicle Excise Duty (car tax) and fuel efficiency **119**.24

vehicles, recycling **161**.23

venison consumption **140**.15

verbal abuse

of children with learning difficulties **165**.15

homophobic **165**.13

shouting at children **179**.39

verbal defensiveness **170**.13

Verified Emission Reductions (VERs) **151**.22

vicarious liability for racism at work **115**.12

victimization **153**.38

and racism **115**.7-8

at work **115**.11-12

victims of abuse

blamed for abuse **155**.2, 3

male **155**.12-13

reasons for not leaving **155**.5, 6, 7

reluctance to speak out **155**.3-4, 30-31

support for **155**.6-7, 28-9

victims of bullying

experiences **165**.2, 5, 10, 14, 15, 16, 17

helping **165**.6, 7-8

victims of crime

racial identity **115**.10

victim-offender mediation **177**.31

video games

age ratings **196**.17

and body image **170**.27

Video Recordings Act 1984 **196**.14

video sharing sites **142**.35

videos

abusive **165**.31

onine **158**.21-2

see also films

violence

against children **167**.36-9

against girls **154**.13-14

and computer games **158**.33

at football grounds **198**.13

and life on the streets **189**.27-8

and obscenity law **196**.22

and young people **176**.4

see also corporal punishment; domestic abuse; physical abuse

violent street crime **177**.4-5

violent extremism **147**.33-4

viruses, GM, to kill insects **138**.13-14

vitamins **140**.4

in meat **140**.12

and teenage diet **176**.8-9

vitrification of embryos **178**.22

Vocational Certificate of Education (VCE) **139**.18

vocational degree subjects **139**.38-9

vocational qualifications **139**.4, 18

gender difference **139**.10
at schools **183**.31
see also specialist diplomas
vocational training and age discrimination **159**.9
volatile organic compounds **146**.35
volatile substance abuse *see* solvent abuse
voluntary activity
England **131**.3
gap years **156**.15-19
graduates **185**.31
voluntary euthanasia *see* assisted suicide
voting **131**.16, 17, 18
eligibility to vote **131**.16, 18, 30
lowering voting age **131**.28, 29, 30
reasons for not voting **131**.22
voter apathy **131**.22
voter turnout **131**.19-21
vulnerable people, effect of legalizing euthanasia **152**.6-7

W

wages
and child domestic workers **99**.9, 10
footballers **198**.12
effect of immigration **150**.17
migrant workers **150**.9
minimum wage, young people **183**.28
multinational companies **157**.11
see also earnings; incomes; salaries
WAGs (footballers wives and girlfriends) **198**.15-17
waist measurement and exercise **162**.36
Waitrose, plastic bags **161**.14
Wal-Mart, commercial promotion to children **134**.11-12
Wales
decline in chapel attendance **148**.19
health service **187**.30
homelessness **189**.4
teenage pregnancy **182**.2, 7, 10-11
walking
as alternative to car **119**.25
health benefits of **119**.27

to school **119**.25, 26, 27
see also exercise; pedestrians
walking bus **119**.6, 26
war
and public grief **192**.7-8
on terror **167**.22-3
war-affected children **99**.32-5
and the effects of armed conflict **99**.33
help for **99**.34
problem of **99**.32
testimonials of **99**.33-4
warranties, consumer rights **134**.18-19
waste
amounts **161**.1, 3-5, 22
as animal food **140**.17
collection **161**.6
construction industry **146**.11
definition **161**.1
and energy generation **97**.37, 39; **161**.20, 38, 39
food **161**.4, 10-11, 19
government strategy **161**.20
hazardous **161**.1, 6, 32
incineration **161**.7
reducing waste **161**.18, 19, 20, 38
sorting **161**.25
see also household waste; landfill; litter; organic waste;
recycling
waste hierarchy **161**.7, 18
water companies **88**.31
water consumption
clean water as measure of poverty **160**.28
water filters, recycling **161**.25
water pollution **146**.36
water supplies
freshwater resources **193**.5
and water pollution **146**.36
and water shortages **146**.13
water vapour emissions, aircraft **119**.16
waterboarding **167**.27
wave power **97**.2, 6, 12
wealth
children's perceptions of **149**.9-12

Volume numbers appear first (in bold) followed by page numbers; a change in volume number is preceded by a semi-**colon.**

Vol. 88 Food and Nutrition
Vol. 97 Energy Matters
Vol. 99 Exploited Children
Vol. 100 Stress and Anxiety
Vol. 119 Transport Trends
Vol. 129 Gambling Trends
Vol. 134 Customers and Consumerism
Vol. 138 A Genetically Modified Future?
Vol. 139 The Education Problem
Vol. 140 Vegetarian and Vegan Diets
Vol. 141 Mental Health
Vol. 142 Media Issues
Vol. 144 The Cloning Debate
Vol. 146 Sustainability and Environment
Vol. 147 The Terrorism Problem
Vol. 148 Religious Beliefs
Vol. 149 A Classless Society?
Vol. 150 Migration and Population
Vol. 151 Climate Change
Vol. 152 Euthanasia and the Right to Die
Vol. 153 Sexual Orientation and Society
Vol. 154 The Gender Gap
Vol. 155 Domestic Abuse

Vol. 156 Travel and Tourism
Vol. 157 The Problem of Globalisation
Vol. 158 The Internet Revolution
Vol. 159 An Ageing Population
Vol. 160 Poverty and Exclusion
Vol. 161 Waste Issues
Vol. 162 Staying Fit
Vol. 163 Drugs in the UK
Vol. 164 The AIDS Crisis
Vol. 165 Bullying Issues
Vol. 166 Marriage and Cohabitation
Vol. 167 Our Human Rights
Vol. 168 Privacy and Surveillance
Vol. 169 The Animal Rights Debate
Vol. 170 Body Image and Self-Esteem
Vol. 171 Abortion – Rights and Ethics
Vol. 172 Racial and Ethnic Discrimination
Vol. 173 Sexual Health
Vol. 174 Selling Sex
Vol. 175 Citizenship and Participation
Vol. 176 Health Issues for Young People
Vol. 177 Crime in the UK
Vol. 178 Reproductive Ethics

Vol. 179 Tackling Child Abuse
Vol. 180 Money and Finances
Vol. 181 The Housing Issue
Vol. 182 Teenage Conceptions
Vol. 183 Work and Employment
Vol. 184 Understanding Eating Disorders
Vol. 185 Student Matters
Vol. 186 Cannabis Use
Vol. 187 Health and the State
Vol. 188 Tobacco and Health
Vol. 189 The Homeless Population
Vol. 190 Coping with Depression
Vol. 191 The Changing Family
Vol. 192 Bereavement and Grief
Vol. 193 Endangered Species
Vol. 194 Responsible Drinking
Vol. 195 Alternative Medicine
Vol. 196 Censorship Issues
Vol. 197 Living with Disability
Vol. 198 Sport and Society
Vol. 199 Self-Harming and Suicide

inequality **149**.19, 22, 27
    and segregation **115**.32
    and teenage drinking **194**.24
weapons
    and crime **177**.15-16, 29-30
    and the law **177**.7, 30
    and sentences **177**.38-9
    young people's concerns **177**.15-16
weather patterns and climate change **97**.1
Web 2.0 **158**.6
webmail **158**.3
websites
    blocking **196**.38
    and bullying **165**.24
    and child sexual abuse **179**.17
    promoting eating disorders **184**.25-7
    and self-harm **199**.19
    selling repossessed properties **181**.7
    terrorist **147**.8-9
wedding costs **134**.25
weight *see* body weight; obesity
weight loss
    drug treatment **162**.2-3, 6, 20
    and exercise **162**.20, 36
    financial incentives **162**.22-3
    and lifestyle changes **162**.20
    as sign of eating disorder **184**.30
    surgery **162**.3
weight management **176**.7
weight monitoring in schools **162**.16
weight problems *see* obesity; underweight people
weisure **183**.19
welfare support *see* state benefits
well-being, teaching **170**.14-15
whales
    hunting **193**.1
    impact of climate change **193**.29
wheelchairs **197**.11
    wheelchair sport **198**.20-21
Whitehouse, Mary **196**.25-6
WHO (World Health Organization), warnings about
    homeopathy **195**.30-31
wholegrain foods **88**.15
WiFi hijacking **158**.37
wild animals
    as food **140**.17
    and the fur trade **169**.5, 6, 8
    reintroduction in Britain **193**.33-4
wildlife
    butterflies, Britain **193**.36
    conservation **88**.32, 34; **146**.33
    illegal souvenirs **156**.32
    impact of chemicals **193**.16-17
    impact of non-native species **193**.12, 38-9
    London **193**.35
    reintroduction of species, Britian **193**.33
    species loss, England **193**.31-2
    trade **146**.34; **193**.20-21
    see also conservation; endangered species; extinction
wills **192**.24, 25-7
    living *see* advance directives

wind energy **97**.2, 4, 5, 6, 9, 21, 38
    and climate change **97**.15
    costs of **97**.16
    energy available from **97**.5
    new wind farm projects **97**.5
    and noise **97**.17
    numbers of wind farms **97**.11
    offshore **97**.12, 16, 26
    opposition to wind farms **97**.12
    public attitudes to **97**.16
    top myths about **97**.15-17
    turbines **97**.5, 15, 17, 38
    in the UK **97**.13, 26
Windows 7 **158**.22-3
winter deaths, older people **159**.4
wireless networks **158**.5
withdrawal symptoms
    gambling **129**.30
withdrawing or withholding treatment **152**.3, 5-6
wives and girlfriends of footballers (WAGS) **198**.15-17
wolves, reintroduction into Britain **193**.33, 34
Womankind Worldwide **165**.10
womb damage and fertility **178**.4
women
    and abortion
        abortion to save mother's life **171**.22
        right to choose **171**.28
        right to life **171**.17
        views on abortion time limit **171**.29
    and ageing population **159**.5
    and alcohol **194**.7, 14
        increasing consumption **176**.14
        pregnant women **194**.14
    aspiring to be WAGS **198**.15-17
    and body image *see* body image, women
    credit card usage, global **180**.19
    dieting, effect on daughters **184**.21-2
    eating disorders in over 40s **184**.14-15
    equality and child labour **99**.12
    and fertility *see* fertility
    financial implications of partner's death **192**.33
    and financial independence **180**.17-18
    and gambling **129**.21, 34
        online gambling **129**.27
    gender pay gap **154**.2-3, 6, 30, 35-9
    glass cliff/glass ceiling **154**.34, 38
    and globalisation **157**.4
    graduate salaries **139**.36
    and HIV/AIDS **96**.20, 24-5, 29, 30-1; **164**.5-6
        in pregnancy **164**.3, 25, 27, 29-30, 31
    and household finance roles **180**.18-19
    Internet usage **158**.4
    marriage expectations **166**.3
    marriage risks **166**.11
    maternity leave **183**.18, 21, 23, 24
    and mental ill-health **141**.1
    and migration **150**.2, 15
    older women and IVF **178**.17, 19-20
    and online shopping **134**.16
    post-natal depression **190**.2, 14-15, 21-2
    and poverty **160**.15, 25

pregnant women **88**.7
   and smoking **188**.11, 30-32
prisoners, self-harm **199**.12
and sexually transmitted infections (STIs) **96**.3, 9
size zero aspirations **170**.20
and smoking **188**.1, 3, 15
   in pregnancy **188**.11, 30-32
social mobility **149**.21
sperm creation **144**.29
and stress **100**.13
   frequent worrying **100**.19
see also girls and young women; mothers; pregnancy;
   working mothers
women in the workforce **149**.21; **154**.29-34
   effect of children on career **183**.21
   equal pay *see* gender pay gap
   European Union **154**.33
   glass ceiling **154**.38
   glass cliff **154**.34
   in the media **154**.11
   mothers preferring not to work **183**.25
   non-traditional careers **154**.31-2
   in senior positions **154**.17, 29, 34; **183**.12
   see also working mothers
wood, recycling **161**.25
woodland planting on landfill sites **161**.33
words to describe racial identity **115**.4-5
work
   effects of cannabis use **186**.10
   effect on fathers' involvement with children **191**.33
   gambling at work **129**.22-4
   and homelessness **189**.33
     Big Issue selling **189**.37-9
   and mobile phones **158**.13
   past retirement age **159**.10, 15
   see also child labour; employment; migrant workers; slavery
work experience and specialist diplomas **139**.24, 25
work and gender *see* gender and work
work-family balance, fathers **191**.34-5
work-from home scams **134**.27
work intensity, EU **154**.18
work-life balance **154**.30; **183**.16-17, 22-3

see also hours of work
Work Permit System **150**.23
work-related stress **183**.6-7
work-rich and work-poor families **149**.28
work-to-live cycle **180**.23
Worker Registration Scheme (WRS) **150**.6
workforce monitoring by GPS **168**.27
Working Better project **183**.27
working class **149**.3
   attitudes to money **149**.19-20
   attitudes to moving home **149**.26
working conditions
   garment industry **157**.27-9
   international companies **157**.11
   migrants **150**.19, 20
working hours *see* hours of work
working mothers **154**.29; **191**.36
   maternity rights **191**.37-8
   preferring not to work **183**.25
   and social housing **181**.10
working parents **191**.30-39
working poor **160**.5
workplace
   absences **183**.8, 9
   age discrimination **159**.8-13
   and disabled people **197**.20-21, 24-5, 26-7
   exercise **162**.23, 24
   gambling **129**.22-4
   gender gap **154**.17-18
   obesity discrimination **162**.21
   monitoring **168**.9, 38
   racism **115**.11-14
   stress **165**.34
   travel plans **119**.32-3
workplace bullying **165**.32-9
   anti-bullying strategies **165**.35-6, 38
   costs **165**.39
   cyberbullying **165**.37-8
   e-mail **165**.38-9
   effects **165**.34, 35
   extent of **165**.33, 35

Volume numbers appear first (in bold) followed by page numbers; a change in volume number is preceded by a semi-**colon.**

Vol. 88 Food and Nutrition
Vol. 97 Energy Matters
Vol. 99 Exploited Children
Vol. 100 Stress and Anxiety
Vol. 119 Transport Trends
Vol. 129 Gambling Trends
Vol. 134 Customers and Consumerism
Vol. 138 A Genetically Modified Future?
Vol. 139 The Education Problem
Vol. 140 Vegetarian and Vegan Diets
Vol. 141 Mental Health
Vol. 142 Media Issues
Vol. 144 The Cloning Debate
Vol. 146 Sustainability and Environment
Vol. 147 The Terrorism Problem
Vol. 148 Religious Beliefs
Vol. 149 A Classless Society?
Vol. 150 Migration and Population
Vol. 151 Climate Change
Vol. 152 Euthanasia and the Right to Die
Vol. 153 Sexual Orientation and Society
Vol. 154 The Gender Gap
Vol. 155 Domestic Abuse

Vol. 156 Travel and Tourism
Vol. 157 The Problem of Globalisation
Vol. 158 The Internet Revolution
Vol. 159 An Ageing Population
Vol. 160 Poverty and Exclusion
Vol. 161 Waste Issues
Vol. 162 Staying Fit
Vol. 163 Drugs in the UK
Vol. 164 The AIDS Crisis
Vol. 165 Bullying Issues
Vol. 166 Marriage and Cohabitation
Vol. 167 Our Human Rights
Vol. 168 Privacy and Surveillance
Vol. 169 The Animal Rights Debate
Vol. 170 Body Image and Self-Esteem
Vol. 171 Abortion – Rights and Ethics
Vol. 172 Racial and Ethnic Discrimination
Vol. 173 Sexual Health
Vol. 174 Selling Sex
Vol. 175 Citizenship and Participation
Vol. 176 Health Issues for Young People
Vol. 177 Crime in the UK
Vol. 178 Reproductive Ethics

Vol. 179 Tackling Child Abuse
Vol. 180 Money and Finances
Vol. 181 The Housing Issue
Vol. 182 Teenage Conceptions
Vol. 183 Work and Employment
Vol. 184 Understanding Eating Disorders
Vol. 185 Student Matters
Vol. 186 Cannabis Use
Vol. 187 Health and the State
Vol. 188 Tobacco and Health
Vol. 189 The Homeless Population
Vol. 190 Coping with Depression
Vol. 191 The Changing Family
Vol. 192 Bereavement and Grief
Vol. 193 Endangered Species
Vol. 194 Responsible Drinking
Vol. 195 Alternative Medicine
Vol. 196 Censorship Issues
Vol. 197 Living with Disability
Vol. 198 Sport and Society
Vol. 199 Self-Harming and Suicide

preventing **165**.37

signs of **165**.32, 25-6, 27

what to do **165**.32

World Anti-Doping Agency (WADA) **198**.31, 32

World Bank **157**.8, 10, 17

help for developing countries in financial crisis **180**.1-2

World Cup, effect on mental health **141**.23

world food supply, and GM crops **138**.9, 10, 34-5

World Health Organisation (WHO), warnings about homeopathy **195**.30-31

world trade *see* international trade

World Trade Organization (WTO) **88**.33; **157**.2-3, 8, 13-14, 17, 21-4

World Wide Web (www) **158**.2-3

worship **148**.1

see also religion

Y

Y Vote Mock Local elections **131**.27

Yahoo!, semantic web **158**.25-6

Yellow Pages, recycling **161**.26

YMCA, homelessness projects **189**.22

yoga

and back pain **162**.33-4

and exam stress **100**.5

young children

body image **184**.27

gender differences in achievements **154**.23

young offenders **177**.11-12

young parents **182**.14-18

housing rights **189**.25

young people

and age discrimination **159**.12

attitudes to biotechnology **138**.16

attitudes to gun and knife crime **177**.15-16

attitudes to HIV **164**.18

attitudes to marriage **166**.1-2

attitudes to mental ill-health **141**.25

attitudes to police **177**.15-16

and body image **170**.17; **184**.17-18

and the Budget **180**.24

and cannabis **163**.9, 30

anti-drug helpline criticised **186**.26-7

effect on families **186**.23-5

mental health effects **186**.10, 29

penalties for possession **186**.1-2, 5, 9, 30

worldwide use **186**.19

and citizenship *see* young people and citizenship

and cosmetic surgery **170**.32-3, 36

and crime *see* young offenders; youth crime

and criminal justice system **177**.16-18

and debt **134**.24

and depression **190**.25-30

and disability **197**.16-17, 36-7

and domestic abuse **155**.21, 26; **179**.19

and drug abuse **163**.3, 9, 15-16, 18-19; 26-30; **176**.18

eating disorders **184**.21-2, 30-31

and employment **180**.20

fear of **177**.3, 22

financial problems **180**.34-6

and gambling **129**.1

gambling addiction **129**.25, 31, 32-3

National Lottery **129**.11-13

signs of problem gambling **129**.38

views on gambling **129**.13

gang membership **177**.12-14; **189**.28

and gender violence **155**.21

and grief **192**.9-23

and healthy eating **88**.4; **176**.8-9

and HIV/AIDS **96**.17, 24-9, 38; **164**.18

homelessness **189**.21-32

statistics **189**.21, 23

housing

choosing to rent **181**.33

housing rights **189**.24-5

living with parents **181**.4

student housing **181**.18, 19-20

improving profile of young people **177**.21

and the Internet **158**.27

online gaming addiction **158**.39

online risks **158**.28

leaving home, reasons **189**.24, 25, 26, 27

media habits **142**.38

media representation **142**.15

and mental health **176**.29-39; **190**.27

and mental illness **141**.25

and money **180**.20-39

financial awareness **180**.20-22

financial education **180**.37-9

financial outlook **180**.23

financial problems **180**.34-6

pension planning **159**.21

Muslims

and fundamentalist beliefs **147**.16-17

help to reject extremism **147**.34

and multi-faith environments **148**.32-3

news awareness **142**.32

not in employment, education or training (NEET) **183**.32

and nutrition **176**.8-9

parenthood *see* teenage parents

and the police **177**.15-16

and politics *see* young people and citizenship

poverty and mental illness **141**.22

and pregnancy *see* teenage pregnancies

relationships and domestic violence **179**.19

and religion **148**.34

rights **167**.28-39

and self-harm **176**.33-5

sexual exploitation of teenagers **99**.20-2

and sexual health **176**.21-8

and sexually transmitted infections (STIs) **96**.3, 4, 8-9, 25; **176**.24-6

and smoking **176**.3, 4, 12-13; **188**.24-8

stopping smoking **188**.13-14

and social exclusion **149**.38-9

sport and self-esteem **170**.39

and suicide **199**.21, 28, 31-3

teenage girls

breast augmentation **170**.32-3

and domestic violence **155**.26